Raising Boys

Raising Boys

THIRD EDITION

**Why Boys Are Different—and How to Help Them
Become Happy and Well-Balanced Men**

Steve Biddulph

Illustrations by Paul Stanish

TEN SPEED PRESS
Berkeley

Published in the United States by Ten Speed Press, an imprint of
the Crown Publishing Group, a division of Random House, LLC,
a Penguin Random House Company, New York.
www.crownpublishing.com
www.tenspeed.com

Ten Speed Press and the Ten Speed Press colophon are registered trademarks
of Random House, LLC

Editions of this work were previously published in Australia by Finch Publishing, Warriewood,
in 1997, 2003, 2008, and 2013, and subsequently in the United States by Celestial Arts, an
imprint of Ten Speed Press, Berkeley, a division of Random House, LLC, New York, in 1998
and 2008.

The author gratefully acknowledges the permission of the following for the right to reproduce
copyright material in this publication: "What Fathers Do," by Jack Kammer, is reprinted
from *Full Time Dads*, May/June 1995, with the permission of the author. The segment of the
article, "Mid School Crisis," by Jane Figgis, is reproduced with the permission of the *Sydney
Morning Herald*.

We are grateful to the following people for their assistance in providing photographs for this
book: Paul and Judi Taylor, Narelle Sonter, Jim and Jenny Smith, Elia and Tony Wallace, Geoff
and Chris Price, Glenda Downing, Chris and Tony Collins, Catherine James and Bruce Stephens,
Ella and David Martin, Steve and Shaaron Biddulph, Glenys and Brian Atack, Steve and
Henrietta Miller, Miles and Jane Felstead, Suzanne Jensen and Ral Lewis, Wendy Pettit
and Currembeena School, Robert and Sue Holloway, Dave Hancock, and Tony James.

Library of Congress Cataloging-in-Publication Data
Biddulph, Steve.
  Raising boys : why boys are different-and how to help them become happy and well-balanced
men / Steve Biddulph ; illustrations by Paul Stanish. — Third edition.
    pages cm
  Includes bibliographical references and index.
1. Boys—United States—Life skills guides. 2. Boys—United States—Conduct of life.
3. Parenting—United States. 4. Mothers and sons—United States. 5. Fathers and sons—
United States. I. Title.
  HQ775.B53 2013
  305.2308110973—dc23

                        2013047075

Trade paperback ISBN: 978-1-60774-602-7
eBook ISBN: 978-1-60774-603-4

Printed in the United States of America

Cover design by Steve Miller/Snapper Graphics and Colleen Cain
Interior design by Greene Design
Interior illustrations by Paul Stanish
Typesetting by Colleen Cain

10 9 8 7 6 5 4 3 2 1

Third Edition

Contents

Preface to the Third Edition

Ten years ago, boys were often seen as a problem. Too noisy, too energetic, slow learners, poor communicators, a danger to everyone, and then they turn into—men! But those of us who worked with parents and their boys—or had boys of our own and loved them dearly—knew this wasn't right. Important truths needed to be rediscovered. Boys were different, in important ways. New research was telling us some remarkable things about boys' brains and bodies. And by understanding their psychology, their stages and development, their hormones and hard-wired natures, we could raise them to be fine young men: safe, caring, passionate, and purposeful.

The first edition of this book took off around the globe like wildfire. In Australia, New Zealand, the UK, Germany, Brazil, and Japan, it was a best seller, but more than that, it was beloved. It was kept on bedside tables, dog-eared and much visited. People urged their friends to read it. Women nudged their husbands in bed and said, "Listen to this . . ."

Boys have real dangers in their lives. They are three times more likely to die before the age of twenty-one, and five times more likely to have problems at school compared with girls. Millions of boys have poor life chances because we have failed to understand and love them.

But with the new realization of boys' needs—for exercise, for warm and firm relationships with mothers, for fathers and other good men in their lives to be active and engaged, for schools that know how to teach in boy-friendly ways—we can save them still. We can raise a generation of boys who are happier, more alive, more connected to the human race, just in time for a world that so badly needs good men.

Boys are fun. They make you laugh. They are full of life and can share that energy with you. They also touch your heart; they are deeply feeling. So we have tried to put all those qualities into this book as well. Whether your son is a tiny baby, a schoolboy, or a teenager surging with hormones and hopes, this book has something for you. I wish you much joy.

Steve Biddulph

CHAPTER ONE

What Is It with Boys?

Last night, I drove into town for a meeting, or at least tried to, and the situation with young men was once again thrust into my face. Three cars ahead of me, the highway was blocked. A sedan, driven by a seventeen-year-old boy with four friends in the car, had attempted to pull out into traffic but miscalculated. A truck coming up behind had hit the car and carried it fifty yards along the road, badly crushing the vehicle in the impact. Soon, the emergency vehicles arrived: fire, rescue, police, ambulance. Men worked in teams, calmly but rapidly dealing with the situation.

The young driver, unconscious, was gradually cut out of the wreck. His four male passengers had varying injuries, some serious. An older woman, perhaps the mother of one of the boys, came running from a nearby farm. A policeman gently comforted her.

Maleness was everywhere—inexperience and risk on the one side; competence, caring, and steadiness on the other.

It kind of summed up for me the male situation. Men, when they turn out well, are wonderful—selfless, heroic, hardworking. But being young and male is a condition so vulnerable, so prone to disaster. When we see a boy born these days, we can't help wondering—how will he turn out?

Boys at Risk

Thirty years ago, it was girls everyone worried about. Across the world, a huge and spirited effort was mounted to raise the horizons of girls, to give them confidence that they could do anything they wanted with their lives, and to demolish the barriers to their achievement. And it's working; today, it's the girls who are more sure of themselves, motivated, and capable. More girls than boys finish school, more girls go on to college, and they get better grades than boys do.

Parents of daughters find that they are focused and clearheaded, and know where they are going. Boys, in comparison, often don't have a clue. They seem to be adrift in life; failing at school; awkward in relationships; at risk for violence, alcohol, and drugs.

The differences start early—visit any preschool and see for yourself. The girls work together happily; the boys gallop and whoop around. They annoy the girls and fight with each other. In elementary school, the boys are easily distracted and often struggle to keep up. Teachers spend all their time subduing the boys, and the girls miss out on attention. By the time they reach third grade, most boys don't read books any more. Many speak in one-word sentences: "Huh?" "Awwww-yeaaah!" In high school they don't participate in debating, concerts, student councils, or any nonsports activity. They pretend not to care about anything.

In the relationships department, teenage boys are quite unsure about girls and how to get along with them. Some become painfully shy; others are aggressive and unpleasant. They seem to lack even the most basic conversation skills.

And the bottom line, the thing that puts a knot in our stomachs as parents, is of course safety. Between the ages of fifteen and twenty-five, boys are three times more likely than girls to die, usually from accidents, violence, and suicide. Three times more likely to die! And for every boy who dies on the road, ten more are left brain damaged or wheelchair bound, the hidden casualties. Every parent of a son feels that fear when their teenage son goes out with his friends—will he come home safe and sound?

The Good News

That's enough of the bad news. What we all want is young men who are happy, creative, confident, safe, thoughtful, and kind. That's all! We want our boys to turn into fine young men who will be part of the solutions of the twenty-first century. And in the meantime, we need them to do the dishes and tidy their rooms!

In the past ten years, a huge amount has been learned about the true nature of boys—information that may surprise and delight you. We think this book will be a great relief for you to read. For thirty years it was fashionable to say that boys and girls were really just the same. But as parents and teachers kept telling us, this approach wasn't working. Vast amounts of new brain research is confirming parents' intuitions about boys being different in positive ways. We are beginning to understand how to *appreciate* their masculinity—in whatever form it takes—and shape it into something good—not just squash it down.

In this book we will look at many breakthrough areas of understanding boys. In chapter 2 we'll explain their *three distinct stages* of development:

- Birth to six—the *learning to love* years
- Six to fourteen—the time when fathers count most
- Fourteen to adult—when boys need mentors and adults who care, *in addition* to their parents

By knowing these stages you will be prepared and more relaxed about what is coming next and how to deal with it in your son's life.

In chapter 3, we'll examine the effects of *hormones* on boys' behavior, and how to help them ride these powerful waves of development. Everyone knows about hormones, but when do they actually come into action? What effect do they have? Why are thirteen-year-olds often dopey, and fourteen-year-olds so argumentative? And how do you handle this with understanding and keep your sense of humor?

In chapter 4, we'll share some significant new findings about the ways in which boys' *brains* are vulnerable, and how to stimulate a boy's brain so he can link up the left and right sides in order to be good at communication. Because when you chatter, interact, and tell stories to babies, toddlers, and school-age boys, you're actually building their neural linkages so they will become men who are good with words and feelings. The world doesn't need men who can wrestle bears so much these days; it needs men who can connect well with people.

In chapter 5, we address the vital place of *fathers*. Most men, it seems, want to improve on the way their fathers were but don't always know how. We will give you some clues. The fatherhood revolution is one of the most positive developments in the past thirty years. If you are a single mother reading this, we will also tell you what you can do to ensure that your son has good men in his life.

In chapter 6 come some stories and clues about the vital relationship between *mothers* and sons. Mothers need to be confident and proactive with their boys, helping them acquire people skills and feel okay around the opposite sex. A mom is a "practice girlfriend," and she teaches a boy how to get along happily with women. Whether she knows it or not, she is setting the pattern for all his future relationships.

PRACTICAL HELP

Good News about Boys

There's some exciting and encouraging news about today's boys that will interest every parent of a son. In 2007 the U.S. government released a large interagency report on the state of America's children, drawing on the resources of departments from Education to Justice to the Census. The picture confirmed what experts on boys had suspected and what parents had been telling us for years. Things had gotten very bad for boys, but now they were getting better.

The report found that "an alarming decline in the performance of America's boys" had taken place during the 1980s and 1990s. Drug abuse, violent crime, suicide, and sexual promiscuity had all increased, and school performance—which had never been great for boys—had further decreased, while girls were soaring ahead.

Then, in the late 1990s (the time when psychologists and educators began efforts to do something positive about boys), this trend started to reverse. Now boys are in some cases doing better than they ever have. So we have both a cause for celebration and reason to do much more.

First, the bad news . . .

Suicide: American boys are still five times as likely to take their own lives as American girls are.

Education: Girls outnumber boys going to college by four to three.

Girls also outnumber boys finishing high school (but both are getting better at this).

Health: The number of obese boys has risen by 400 percent since the 1970s. Junk food and lack of exercise is harming our boys.

The good news . . .

Crime: Juvenile crime has been reduced by two-thirds since 1993. The number of juvenile boys in prison has halved.

Drugs: The number of high school boys using drugs has halved since 1980.

Alcohol: Heavy drinking among boys—measured as having five drinks in a row at least once in the previous two weeks—is now the lowest on record. (Though it's still around two in ten boys.)

Sex: Ten percent fewer high school boys and girls are sexually active than in the 1990s. Among sexually active teens, seven in ten use condoms, compared with five in ten in the 1990s. Rates of teen pregnancy and abortions are lower than they have ever been.

Employment: Youth unemployment has fallen by a quarter since the 1980s. Black young men have improved the most. In 1984 one in three young black men ages eighteen and nineteen was unemployed. Today that figure is fewer than one in five.

And the reason is?

Child-focused time, totaled for both parents, was thirteen hours a week in 1965 and had fallen to eleven hours a week in 1985. But it had risen to twenty hours per week in 2005!

Part of the reason is a huge increase in the time children spend with their dads—many of whom have doubled their child-centered activities in the past decade.

One thing we can say for sure to parents and teachers: caring about boys, understanding them better, spending more time with them, pays off. These dramatic changes prove it.

In chapter 7 we'll talk about boys and *sex*—another area that seems to go either really well or really badly for boys.

Because *school* is where boys spend half their lifetimes before adulthood, chapter 8 looks at how we can dramatically improve schools. We consider why it's important that boys don't start school too young, since their brains grow in a different sequence than, and slower than, girls' brains. This information has changed tens of thousands of families' timing on when they send their sons to school or even to daycare. Along with this we will help you decide which teachers and which school will help your boy best.

In chapter 9 we tackle *sports*, which has become a real hazard to boys' bodies and souls—though when done right, sports can be so good for them.

Finally, in chapter 10 we suggest some ways in which the whole *community* can support boys in their journey to becoming men. Parents can't do this without help. Parents need to be making choices, even when their boys are still little babies, that ensure other adults are in place to be there for them as they navigate through their teens. You need a circle of friends and extended family to help a boy make it to adulthood unharmed.

Interested? Mystified? Then it's time to begin.

Boys can be just great. We can make them so. Understanding is the key.

CHAPTER TWO

The Three Stages of Boyhood

Have you ever browsed through a family photo collection and seen photos of a boy taken over the course of many years, from babyhood through to young manhood? If you have, you'll know that boys don't grow up in a smooth way. They go in surges—looking the same for a year or two, then suddenly seeming to change overnight. And that's only on the outside. On the inside, great changes are happening, too. But developing maturity and character aren't as automatic as physical growing. A boy can get stuck. Everyone knows at least one man who is large in body but small in mind or soul. He just hasn't developed as a mature person. Such men are everywhere—they might be rich, powerful, a president, or a tycoon, but you look at them and think, *Yep, still a boy. And not a very nice one.*

Boys don't grow up well if you don't help them. You can't just shovel in cereal, provide clean T-shirts, and expect him to

one day wake up as a man! You need to follow a certain program. The trick is to understand what is needed—and when.

Luckily, boys have been around for a very long time. Every society in the world has encountered the challenge of raising boys and has come up with solutions. The three stages of boyhood are timeless and universal. Native Americans, the San tribe of the Kalahari, Australian Aborigines—all knew about these stages. We know them from science—hormone studies and brain imaging. And from observation—whenever I talk about these stages with parents, they say, "That's right!" because the stages match their experience. They just hadn't thought about it before.

Here are the stages at a glance:

1. The first stage of boyhood is from *birth to six*—the span of time when the boy primarily belongs to his mother. He is "her" boy, even though his father may play a very big role, too. The aim at this age is to give strong love and security, and to "switch a boy on" to life as a warm and welcoming experience.

2. The second stage includes the years from *six to fourteen*—when the boy, out of his own internal drives, starts wanting to learn to be a man, and looks more and more to his father for interest and activity. (Though his mother remains very involved, and the wider world is beckoning, too.) The purpose of this stage is to build competence and skill while developing kindness and playfulness, too—becoming a balanced person. This is the age when a boy becomes happy and secure about being male.

3. Finally, the years from *fourteen to adult*—when the boy needs input from male mentors if he is to complete the journey into being fully grown up. Mom and Dad step back a little, but they must organize some good mentors in their son's life or he will have to rely on an ill-equipped peer group for his sense of self. The aim is for your son to learn skills, responsibility, and self-respect by joining more and more with the adult community.

Please note: These stages do not indicate a sudden or sharp shift from one parent to another.

It's not like there's the mom stage, then the dad stage, and then the mentor stage. For instance, an involved dad can do a huge amount from birth onward, or even take the role a mother usually has if need be. And a mother doesn't quit when a boy reaches six. Quite the opposite. The stages indicate a shift of emphasis: that the father comes to the fore more from six through fourteen, and the importance of mentors increases from fourteen onward. In a sense, it's about adding on the new ingredients at each stage.

The three stages help us know what to do. For example, it's clear that fathers of boys from six to fourteen must not be busy workaholics or absent themselves emotionally or physically from the family. If they do, this will certainly damage their boys. (Yet most fathers of the twentieth century did just that—as many of us remember from our own childhoods.)

The stages tell us that we need to bring in extra help from the community when our sons are in their mid-teens—the role that family members (uncles and grandfathers) or the tradesman-apprentice relationship used to take. Too often, teenagers move outward into the big world but no one is there to catch them, and they spend their teens and early adulthood in a dangerous halfway stage with only peers to depend on.

It's probable that many problems with boys' behavior—poor school motivation, depression, and getting into strife with the law (drunk driving, fighting, crime, and so on)—develop because we haven't known about these stages and haven't provided the right human ingredients at the right times.

The stages are so important that we must look at them in more detail and decide how to respond. That's what we'll do now.

From Birth to Six:
The Gentle Years

Babies are babies. Whether they are a boy or girl is not a concern to them, and needn't be to us either. Babies love to be cuddled, to play, to be tickled, and to giggle—to explore and be swooshed around. Their personalities vary a lot. Some are easy to handle—quiet and relaxed—and sleep long hours. Others are noisy and wakeful, always wanting some action. Some are anxious and fretful, needing lots of reassurance that we are there and that we love them.

What babies and toddlers need most is to form a special bond with at least one person. Usually this person is their mother. Partly because she is the one who is most willing and motivated, partly because (if breastfeeding) she provides the milk, and partly because she tends to be cuddly, restful, and soothing in her approach, a mother is usually best equipped to provide what a baby needs. Her own hormones (especially prolactin—released into her bloodstream as she breastfeeds) prime her to want to be with her child and to give it her full attention.

Except for breastfeeding, dads can provide all a baby needs but tend to do it differently. Studies show them to be more vigorous in their playing; they like to stir children up, whereas mothers like to calm them down. (Though if fathers get as deprived of sleep as mothers sometimes do, they would want to calm them down, too!)

GENDER DIFFERENCES BEGIN TO SHOW

Some gender differences between boys and girls do begin to appear early on. Here are just a few discoveries researchers have made:

- Boy babies are less aware of faces.
- Girl babies have a much better sense of touch.
- The retinas in the back of boys' eyes are differently made, so they see more movement, and less color and texture.
- Boys grow faster than girls and become stronger, yet they are more troubled by separations from their mother.
- Boys in toddlerhood move around more and occupy more space. They like to handle and manipulate objects more—and build high buildings out of blocks, whereas girls prefer low-rise.

- At preschool, boys tend to ignore a new child who arrives in the group, whereas girls will notice them and befriend them.

And sadly, adults tend to treat boys more harshly. Studies have shown that parents hug and cuddle girl children far more, even as newborn babies. They tend to talk less to boy babies. And mothers who use physical punishment are likely to hit boys harder and more often than they do girls.

LEARNING TO LOVE

If a mother is the main care-giver, a boy will see her as his first model for intimacy and love. From toddlerhood on, if she sets limits with her son firmly, but without hitting or shaming him, he will take this in stride. He will want to please her, and he will be easier to manage because the attachment is so strong. He knows he has a special place in her heart. Being made to wait or change his behavior may baffle him, but he will get over it. He knows he's loved, and he will not want to displease the person at the center of his existence.

Her interest and fun in teaching and talking to him helps his brain develop more verbal skills and makes him more sociable. We'll see later that this is important for boys, because they need more help than girls to catch on to social skills.

If a mother is terribly depressed and therefore unresponsive in the first year or two of her son's life, his brain may undergo physical changes to become a "sad brain." If she is constantly angry, hitting or hurting him, he will be confused over whether she loves him. (Please note this is constant anger we are talking about—not occasionally losing it, as happens to all parents. We aren't supposed to be angels as parents, or how would our children learn about the real world?) Those of us who are around young mothers have to be careful to support and help them, ensuring that they are not left isolated or overwhelmed with physical tasks. A mother needs others to augment her life, so that she can relax and do this important work. If we care for young mothers, they can care for their babies. Husbands are the first rank of help, but family and neighbors are also needed.

WHAT GOES ON BETWEEN MOTHER AND BABY BOY?

Science has trouble measuring something like love, but it is getting closer. Researchers studying mothers and babies have observed what they call *joint attention sequences*. This is love in action, love that you can see. When researchers filmed mothers and babies going about their day, they discovered that joint attention sequences happen perhaps fifty or a hundred times a day. You will have certainly experienced this with your own child. The baby seeks out your attention with a gurgle or cry. You look toward it, to see that it is looking at you. The baby is delighted to make eye contact and wiggles with delight. You talk back to it. Maybe you are holding it, or changing it, or maybe the baby is across the room as you work nearby. The exchange goes on, a pre-words conversation; it's delightful and warm.

Another kind of joint attention sequence is when your baby is distressed, and you croon, stroke, or hold it gently, distract it, care for it based on your growing experience of what works to help it calm down. Or you engage with your baby just to enjoy seeing it become happy or excited. Soon your joint attention may be directed at a toy, flower, animal, or noisemaking object that you enthuse about together. You teach your baby to be interested in the world.

This is one of the most significant things parents ever do for their baby. Inside their little heads, their brains are sprouting like a broccoli growing in the springtime. When a baby is happy, growth hormone flows in its body, right into its brain, and development blossoms. When it is stressed, the stress hormone cortisol slows down growth, especially brain growth. So interaction, laughter, and love are like food for a baby's brain. All this interaction is being remembered in these new brain areas; the baby is learning how to read faces and moods, be sensitive, learn calmness, fun, stern admonition, or warm love. Soon the baby will learn language, music, movement, rhythm—but above all, the capacity for feeling good and being empathic with other people. Boy babies are just a little slower, a little less wired for sociability, so they especially need this help. And they need it from someone who knows them very well, has the time, and is reasonably happy and content.

The process keeps going right into little boyhood. A mother shows delight when her son catches lizards or makes mud pies, and she admires his achievements. His father tickles him and play-wrestles with him and is also gentle and nurturing, reading stories and comforting him when he is sick. The little boy learns that men are kind as well as exciting, that men read books, that they are capable in the home. He also learns that mothers are kind—and also practical, worldly, and part of the bigger world.

EARLY DAYCARE IS NOT GOOD FOR BOYS

If at all possible, a boy should stay home with one of his parents or a close relative until about age three. Daycare of the institutional kind does not suit boys' nature during these very early years. Many studies have shown that boys are more prone than girls to separation anxiety and to becoming emotionally shut down as a result of feeling abandoned. Also, a boy of this age may cope with his anxiety by becoming restless or aggressive. Experienced caregivers talk about the "sad/angry boy syndrome"—a little boy who feels abandoned and anxious and converts that into hitting and hurting behavior. He may carry this behavior into school and later life.

Care by a loving relative is far better than an institutional situation for toddlers under three. Children under three need

to spend the long days of childhood with people to whom they are very special.

IN SHORT

To sum up, the first lessons boys need to learn are in closeness—shown through trust, warmth, fun, and kindness. Under six years of age, gender isn't a big deal, and it shouldn't be made so. Mothers are usually the primary parent, but a father can take this place. What matters is that one or two key people love this child and make him central for these few years. That way, he develops inner security for life, and his brain acquires the skills of intimate communication and a love of life and the world. These years are soon over. Enjoy your little boy while you can!

From Six to Thirteen: Learning to Be Male

At around six years of age, a big change takes place in boys. There seems to be a sudden "switching on" of boys' masculinity at this age. Even boys who have not watched much TV suddenly want to play with swords, wear Superman capes, fight and wrestle, and make lots of noise. Something else happens that is really important: it's been observed in all societies around the world. At around six years of age, little boys seem to "lock on" to their dad, or step-dad, or whichever male is around; they want to be with him, learn from him, and copy him. They want to study how to be male.

If a dad ignores his son at this time, the boy will often launch an all-out campaign to get his attention. Once I consulted in the case of a little boy who repeatedly became seriously ill for no apparent reason. He was placed in intensive care. His father, a leading medical specialist, flew back from a conference overseas to be with him, and the boy got better. The father went away to another conference, and the illness came back. That's when they called in the psychologists. We asked the father to reconsider his lifestyle, which involved being on the road for *eight months a year!* He did this, and the boy has not been ill since.

Boys may steal, break things, act aggressively at school, and develop any number of problem behaviors just to get Dad to take an interest. But if Dad is already in there on a daily basis, playing, teaching, and caring for his son, then this age will go much more smoothly.

MOMS STILL MATTER JUST AS MUCH

This sudden shift of interest to the father does not mean that Mom leaves the picture. In the past, in North America and the UK especially, mothers would often distance themselves from their boys at this age, to "toughen them up." (This was also the age at which the British upper classes sent their boys to boarding school.) But as Olga Silverstein has argued in her book *The Courage to Raise Good Men* (coauthored with Beth Rashbaum), this often backfired. If, in the early years, a mother suddenly withdraws her presence or her warmth and affection, then a terrible thing happens: the boy, to control his grief and pain, shuts down the part of him that connects with her—his tender and loving part. He finds it is just too painful to feel loving feelings if they are no longer reciprocated by his mother. If a boy shuts down this part of himself, he will have trouble as an adult expressing warmth or tenderness to his own partner or children, and be a rather tense and brittle man. We all know men like this (bosses, fathers, even husbands) who are emotionally restricted and awkward with people. We can make sure our sons are not like this by hugging them, talking to them, and listening to their feelings, whether they are five, ten, or fifteen.

Mothers have to stay constant, while being willing to let Dad also play his part. Boys need to know they can count on Mom and don't have to shut off their tender feelings. Things work best if they can stay close to Mom, but add Dad, too. If a dad feels a child is too taken up with his mother's world (which can happen), then he should increase his own involvement—not criticize the mother! Sometimes a dad is too critical or expects too much, and the boy is afraid of him. A father may have to learn to be more thoughtful, gentler, or just more fun if his son is to successfully cross the bridge into manhood with him.

The six-to-fourteen-year-old boy still adores his mother and has plenty to learn from her. But his interests are changing— he is becoming more focused on what men have to offer. A boy knows that he is turning into a man. He has to "download the software" from an available male to complete his development.

The mother's job is to relax about this and stay warm and supportive. The father's job is to progressively step up his involvement. If there is no father around, the child depends more on finding other men—at school, for instance.

IN BRIEF

All through the primary school years and into mid-high school, boys should spend a lot of time with their fathers and mothers, gaining their help, learning how to do things, and enjoying their company. From an emotional viewpoint, the father is now more significant. The boy is ready to learn from his dad, and listens to what he has to say. Often he will take more notice of his father. It's enough to drive a mother wild!

This window of time—from about age six to the fourteenth birthday—is the major opportunity for a father to have an influence on (and build the foundations of masculinity in) his son. Now is the time to "make time." Little things count: playing in the backyard on summer evenings; going for walks, talking about life, and telling him about your own childhood; working on hobbies or sports together for the enjoyment of doing it. This is when good memories are laid down that will nourish your son, and you, for decades to come.

Don't be deterred if your son acts "cool," as he has learned to do this from his schoolmates. Persist and you will find a laughing, playful boy just under the surface. Enjoy this time when he really wants to be with you. By mid-adolescence his interests will pull him more and more into a wider world beyond. All I can do here is plead with you—don't put it off until it's too late!

PRACTICAL HELP

What to Do If You're a Single Parent

For thousands of years single mothers have needed to raise boys without a man in the house. And more often than not these boys have turned out just great.

Over the years I have interviewed mothers who did this, to find out their secret. Successful single mothers of sons always give the same advice. First, they found good male role models, calling in help from uncles, good friends, schoolteachers, sports coaches, youth leaders, and so on (choosing with care to guard against the risk of sexual abuse). A boy needs to "know what a good man looks like." If they have caring men involved enough, and over a long enough period of time, this provides that one thing a mother can't give—a male example to copy. If there are one or two good men who know and care about your son, it makes a huge difference. Single moms can also comfort themselves in knowing that many boys with dads see them for only minutes a day. Whatever you do, don't marry some deadbeat just so your son can have a man in the house! Part of the survival kit of single mothers is the network of good men in their community.

If you are a dad, your son will certainly have friends who don't have dads or whose dads are not very involved. Think about inviting that boy when you plan a trip to a concert, the beach, a sports game, or a weekend away with your own son. His mom will be so appreciative, though she would never have asked for this, not wanting to impose. (She may be a little cautious, so perhaps don't start with a nine-day climb of Mount Dangerous.)

Single parents need to be networked: being involved in a church, sporting group, extended family, or neighborhood where kids are loved and valued is a natural way to provide other good adult role models and people to "bounce off," especially in adolescence.

Single Dads

Single dads are a growing group in society, and we have to admire them for pioneering a role that has barely been recognized up until now.

For dads of daughters, the same challenges occur in reverse. How to find good women for role models, how to both respect and yet support their daughters' passage into puberty, how to build a network of support so that you and your child don't suffer from isolation and the stress this can bring. Dads of sons need to learn the nurturing and tender side of parenthood even more, and in fact single dads are often more well rounded, having realized that they are the emotional support for their kids in a way that is often provided by mothers by default. Parenthood, once embraced, seems to change men in good ways. But with all single parents who are our neighbors and friends, we need to recognize their efforts and offer support and care so that their families don't go under. It takes a village, as they say. At least, it takes a few good friends.

There's one more thing. All the successful single parents I've known also recognized they needed to be kind to themselves and not become long-suffering martyrs. (Martyrhood is like yogurt: it has a shelf life of maybe two weeks, then tends to go kind of sour!) Single parents who did well planned into their lives a massage, game of tennis, yoga class, or time vegging out watching TV when the kids were asleep, and kept this commitment to themselves and their well-being. (For more help on single parenting, see also page 114.)

PRACTICAL HELP

Five Fathering Essentials

All fathers have one thing in common: they would like to be good dads. The problem is, if we weren't given great fathering ourselves—and many of us weren't—how do you turn good intentions into action? The best way is to hang around other men and learn from what they do, what you would copy, and what you would never repeat! From talking to hundreds of men, here are five basic clues:

1. **Start early.** Be involved in the pregnancy—talk with your partner about your hopes for the child, your plans and dreams for how you want your family to be. Plan to be at the birth—and stick to the plan! Go to some birth classes, especially those just for fathers, which are starting to be offered more and more. Once your baby is born, get involved in baby care right from the start. Have a specialty. Bathing is good; they are slippery little suckers, but it's a fun time and a big help.

   This is the key time for relationship building. Caring for a baby "primes" you hormonally and alters your life priorities. Fathers who physically care for their babies start to get fascinated and very in tune with them—it's called *engrossment*. You can become the expert at getting babies back to sleep in the middle of the night—walking them, bouncing, singing gently, or whatever works for you! Don't settle for being a klutz around babies—keep at it, and get support and advice from the baby's mother and other experienced friends. And take pride in your ability.

2. **Make time.** Some men work in incredibly family-hostile workplaces or careers—where the demands of the job or employer mean they spend months away (for instance in the military) or commute or travel and may not see their baby or toddler for days at a time. We have to be honest here: this truly endangers the connection with your child and also endangers the

mental health of the mother, unless she has wonderful support. Next time you're offered a "promotion" involving longer hours and more nights away from home, seriously consider telling your boss, "Sorry, my kids come first."

3. **Show your love.** Hugging, holding, and playing tickling and wrestling games can take place right through to adulthood! And do gentler things, too—kids respond to quiet storytelling, sitting together, singing, or playing music. Tell your kids how great, beautiful, creative, and intelligent they are (often, and with feeling). If your parents were not demonstrative, you will just have to learn.

   Some men fear that cuddling their son will make him a "sissy" (for which you can read "gay"). It won't. In fact, the opposite is occasionally true. Many gay or bisexual men I have spoken to say that a lack of fatherly affection was part of what made male affection more important to them. For both sons and daughters, a dad's affection is vital. A child can't understand that you work long hours, worry over tax forms, or scrimp and save for their future, because *that's not something they can see or touch.* Kids know they are loved through touch and eye contact and laughter and fun. Affection is reassuring; it conveys love in a way that words cannot. Children who are hugged and kissed by their mothers feel safer in the world, and when Dad does it too they are doubly secure.

4. **Lighten up.** Enjoy your kids. Being with them out of guilt or obligation is second-rate; they sense you are not really there in spirit. Experiment to find those activities that you both enjoy. Take the pressure to achieve off your kids—when you play a sport or game, don't get into too much heavy coaching or competition. Remember to laugh and goof around. Enroll them in only one or at most two organized sports or activities, so they have time to just "be." Reduce "racing around"

time and devote it instead to walks, just-for-fun games, and conversations. Avoid overcompetitiveness in any activity beyond what is good fun.

5. **Heavy down.** Some fathers today are lightweight "good-time" dads who leave all the hard stuff to their partners. After a while of this, women start to feel like—and say—"I have three kids, and one of them is my husband." There is an unmistakable indicator for this—when your sex life declines badly! Get involved in the decisions and discussions in the kitchen, help supervise homework, and do some housework. Develop methods of discipline that are calm but definite. Don't hit— although with young children you may have to gently hold and restrain them from time to time. Don't shout if you can help it. Aim to be the person who stays calm and keeps things on track. You are in charge through your clarity, not through being bigger and meaner. Do listen to your children and take their feelings into account. You are on a gradient, from being totally in charge of a baby or toddler to being on an equal footing with a twenty-one-year-old who pays for dinner.

Talk with your partner about the big picture: "How are we doing overall? What changes are needed?" Parenting as a team can add a new bond between you and your partner. Check with your partner if you are stuck or don't know how to react. You don't have to have all the answers. Parenthood is about making mistakes, fixing them, and moving right along.

PRACTICAL HELP

When Boys Are Short

Parents sometimes worry if their son is not growing as tall as other boys. Indications are that this worry is needless. A 1994 study of 180 boys and 78 girls, aged eight to fourteen, who were sufficiently short to be referred to a special center for assessment, found that short children are no more likely to be maladjusted than taller children.

Earlier research suggested shorter youngsters were more likely to be shy, anxious, or depressed, but times have changed, and more recent studies have not found this to be so. Society today is more diverse and human differences are more valued. If a child is praised and valued, and has good communication within the family, then being different is much less likely to cause stress.

In one study, short boys described themselves as less socially active but did not have more behavior problems than boys of average height. Girls in the study often had even better mental health than girls of normal height. Children whose parents were short themselves seemed to have far fewer problems, probably because of the good role modeling their parents provided. These parents were less likely to be worried or seek medical help for shortness.

In the United States to date twenty thousand children have taken human growth hormone to overcome shortness, a treatment costing tens of thousands of dollars. Doctors recommend the hormone treatment only if it is medically necessary, such as when kidney failure or other conditions have caused a deficiency in the growth hormone. Pediatricians do not believe that psychological reasons are sufficient to justify the treatment, which is painful and inconvenient and "can do more harm than good."

Fourteen and Onward:
Becoming a Man

At around age fourteen a new stage begins. Usually by now the boy is growing fast and a remarkable thing is happening on the inside—his testosterone levels have increased by almost 800 percent!

Although every boy is different, it's common for boys at this age to get a little argumentative, restless, and moody. It's not that they are turning bad—it's just that they are being born into a new self, and birth always involves some struggle. They are needing to find answers to big questions, to begin new adventures and challenges, and to learn competencies for living—and their body clocks are urging them on.

I believe this is the age when we fail kids the most. In our society all we offer the mid-teens is more of the same: more school, more of the routines of home. But the adolescent is hungry for something more. He is hormonally and physically ready to break into an adult role, but we want him to wait another five or six years! It's little wonder that problems arise.

What's needed is something that will engage the spirit of a boy—pull him headlong into some creative effort or passion that gives his life wings. Many of the things that parents have nightmares about (adolescent risk-taking, alcohol, drugs, and criminal activity) happen because we do not find channels for young men's desire for glory and heroic roles. Boys look out at the larger society and see little to believe in or join with. Even their rebellion is packaged up and sold back to them in the form of advertisements and products of the music industry.

They want to jump somewhere better and higher but that place is nowhere in sight.

WHAT OLD SOCIETIES DID

In every society before ours—from the tropics to the poles—in every time and place anthropologists have studied, the mid-teen boys received a burst of intensive care and attention from the whole community. This was a universal human activity. So it must have been important. These cultures knew something we are still learning—that *parents cannot raise teenage boys without the help of other adults.*

One reason for this is that fourteen-year-old sons and their fathers drive each other crazy. Often it's all a father can do to keep loving his son. Trying to do this *and* teach him can be just impossible. (For the men reading this, remember your dad teaching you to drive?) Somehow the two males get their horns tangled and make each other worse. Fathers just get too intense. They feel they are running out of time; they see their own mistakes being repeated.

Once, when I was a beginning family therapist, I saw a family whose youngest teenage son had run away and lived in the railway yards for several days. He was found, but it scared everyone involved and the family felt they needed to get help. Talking to them, I discovered a remarkable thing. Sean, the runaway, was their youngest son, but he wasn't the first to do this. Each of their three sons had actually run away from home around this age. My boss, a wise and scarily intuitive man, looked the father straight in the eye. "Where did you go when you were fourteen?" The father pretended not to understand, but, with his entire family looking accusingly on at him, he grinned foolishly and spilled the beans. He had been a teenage runaway at fourteen, after huge fights with his dad. He'd never told his wife about this, let alone his kids. As his own sons had each in turn reached this age, the father, without realizing it, had become increasingly impossible, uptight, and picky with them. Effectively, albeit unconsciously, he had driven them to run away. Luckily, the family tradition called for coming home again, safe and sound.

Fathers and fourteen-year-old sons can get a bit tense with each other. If someone else can assist with the male role at this age, dads and sons can relax a little. (Some wonderful movies have been based on this idea—for instance, *Searching for Bobby Fisher*, *Finding Forrester*, and *The Run of the Country*.)

Traditionally, in many diverse societies, two things have been done to help young men into adulthood. First, they were "taken on" and *mentored* into adulthood by one or more men who cared about them and taught them important skills for living. And second, at certain stages of this mentoring process, the community of older men took the young men away and *initiated* them. This meant being put through some serious growing-up processes, including testing, sacred teaching, and new responsibilities. We'll come back to this later in our final chapter on community.

We can contrast the Lakota experience with modern-day sons and their mothers, who (according to writers like Babette Smith in *Mothers and Sons*) often remain in an awkward, distant, or rather infantile relationship for life. Their sons fear getting close and yet, being uninitiated as men, they never really escape. Instead, they relate to all women in a dependent and immature way. Not having entered the community of men, they are distrustful of other men and have few real friends. They are afraid of commitment to women because for

STORIES FROM THE HEART

A Lakota Initiation

The Native American people known as the Lakota were a vigorous and successful society, characterized by especially equal relationships between men and women.

At around the age of fourteen Lakota boys were sent on a "vision quest" or initiation test. This involved sitting and fasting on a mountain peak to await a vision or hallucination brought on by hunger. This vision would include a being who would carry messages from the spirit world to guide the boy's life. As the boy fasted and trembled alone on the peak, he would hear mountain lions snarl and move in the darkness below him. The sounds were actually made by the men of the tribe, keeping watch, to ensure the boy's safety. A young person was too precious to the Lakota to endanger needlessly.

Eventually, when the young man returned to the tribe, his achievement was celebrated. But from that day, for two whole years, *he was not permitted to speak directly to his mother*.

Lakota mothers, like the women of all hunter-gatherer groups, are very close and affectionate with their children, and the children often sleep alongside them in the women's huts and tents. The Lakota believed that if the boy spoke to his mother immediately following his entry into manhood, the pull back into boyhood would be so great that he would "fall" back into the world of women and never grow up.

After the two years had passed, a ceremonial rejoining of the mother and son took place, but by this time he was a man and able to relate to her as such. Women who have heard this story say they found it very moving—it brings both grief and joy. The reward that Lakota mothers gained from this "letting go" is that they were assured their sons would return as respectful and close adult friends.

them it means being mothered, and that means being controlled. They are real "nowhere men."

It's only by leaving the world of women that young men can break the mother mold and relate to women as fellow adults. Domestic violence, unfaithfulness, and the inability to make a marriage work may result not from any problem with women but from men's failure to take boys on this transforming journey.

You might think that in old societies like the Lakota the boys' mothers, and perhaps the fathers too, would resent or fear their son's being taken over by others. But this was not the case. The initiators were men they had known and trusted all their lives. The women understood and welcomed this help, because they sensed the need for it. They were giving up a rather troublesome boy and getting back a more mature and integrated young man. And they were probably very proud of him.

The initiation into adulthood was not a single "weekend special." It could involve months of teaching about how to behave as a man, what responsibilities the initiates were taking on, and where to find strength and direction. The ceremonies we normally hear about were only the marker events. Some of these ceremonies were harsh and frightening (and we would not want to return to these) but overall they were done with purpose and care, and were spoken of with great appreciation by those who had passed through them.

Traditional societies depended for their survival on raising competent and responsible young men. It was a life-and-death issue, never left to chance. They developed very proactive programs for doing this. And the process involved the whole adult community in a concerted effort. (Some innovative ways we might go about this, appropriate to our times, are described in the final chapter, "A Community Challenge.")

IN THE MODERN WORLD

Mentoring today is mostly unplanned and piecemeal, and lots of young men don't receive any mentoring at all. Those doing the mentoring—sports coaches, uncles, teachers, and bosses—rarely understand their role and may do it badly. Mentoring used to happen in the workplace, especially under the apprenticeship system, in which a young man learned a great deal about attitudes and responsibilities along with his trade skills. This has all but disappeared. You won't get much mentoring while stocking shelves at the local supermarket.

ENLISTING THE HELP OF OTHERS

The years from fourteen until the early twenties are for moving into the adult world, for separating from parents. Parents carefully and watchfully ease back. This is the time when a son develops a life that is quite separate from the family. He has teachers you barely know, experiences you never hear about; he faces challenges that you cannot help him with. Pretty scary stuff.

A fourteen- or sixteen-year-old is far from ready to just be "out there." There have to be others to act as a bridge, and this is what mentors do. We should not leave youngsters in a peer group at this age without adult care. But a mentor is more than a teacher or a coach: a mentor is special to the child, and

the child is special to him. A sixteen-year-old will not always listen to his parents—his inclination is not to. But a mentor is different. This is a time for the youngster to make his "glorious mistakes," and part of the mentor's job is to make sure the mistakes are not fatal.

Parents have to ensure that mentoring happens—and they should have a big hand in choosing who does it. It really helps to belong to a strong social group—an active church, a family-minded sport, a community-oriented school, or a group of friends who really care about each other.

You need to have these kinds of friends to provide what uncles and aunts used to—someone close at hand who cares about and enjoys your kids. These friends can show an interest in your youngsters, ask them about their views. Ideally they will make your kids welcome in their homes, "kick their butts" (figuratively speaking) when it's called for, and be a

STORIES FROM THE HEART

The Story of Nat, Stan, and the Motorbike

Nat was fifteen, and his life was not going well. He had always hated school and found writing difficult, and things were just mounting up. The school he went to was a caring school, and his parents, the counselor, and the principal knew each other and could talk comfortably. They met and decided that if Nat could find a job, they would arrange an exemption. Perhaps he was one of those boys who would be happier in the adult world than the in-between world of high school.

Luckily Nat scored a job, in a one-man pizza shop—"Stan's Pizza"—and left school. Stan, who was about thirty-five, had a flourishing business and needed help. Nat went to work there and loved it. His voice deepened, he stood taller, his bank balance grew. His parents, though, began to worry for a new reason. Nat planned to buy a motorbike—a big bike—to get to work. Their home was up a winding, slippery road in the mountains. They watched in horror as his savings got closer to the price of the motorcycle. They suggested a car, to no avail. Time passed.

One day Nat came home and, as teenage boys will, muttered something sideways as he walked past the dinner table. Something about a car.

They asked him to repeat it, not sure if they should.

"Oh, I'm not going to get a bike. I was talking to Stan. Stan reckons a guy'd be an idiot to buy a motorbike, living up here. He reckons I should wait and get a car."

Thank God for Stan! thought his parents, but outwardly they just smiled and went on eating their meal.

listening ear when things at home are a little tense. (Many a mother has experienced a big fight with her teenage daughter, who then runs off to tell her woes to her mom's best friend down the road. This is what friends are for!)

You can do the same for their kids, too. Teenagers are quite enjoyable when they are not your own!

WHAT IF THERE IS NO MENTOR AVAILABLE?

If there are no mentors around, a young man may fall into a lot of potholes on the road to adulthood. He may fight needlessly with his parents in trying to establish himself as independent. He may become withdrawn and depressed. Kids at this age have so many dilemmas and decisions—about sexuality, study choices, what to do about drugs and alcohol. If Mom and Dad spend time with them and are in touch with their world, kids will keep talking to them about these things. But sometimes they need to talk to other adults, too. In one study, it was shown that just one good adult friend outside the family was a significant preventive of juvenile crime. (As long as the friend isn't *into* crime!)

Young men will try their best to find structure and direction in their lives. They may choose a born-again religion or a cult, disappear onto the Internet, follow emo or goth music or dress style, or sports, or gang membership, or surfing. These may be helpful or harmful. The point is, if we don't have a community for kids to belong to, they will make their own. But a community made up of only the peer group is not enough—it may be just a group of lost souls, without the skills or knowledge to help its members. Many boys' friendship

PRACTICAL HELP

Overcoming Boys' Tendency Toward Arrogance

It's possible that boys are naturally prone to a certain degree of arrogance. Until recently, boys were often raised expecting to be waited on by women. In some cultures, boys are still treated like little gods. In today's world, the result can be an obnoxious boy whom no one wants to be around.

It's therefore very important that boys are taught humbleness— through experiences such as having to apologize, having to do work to help others, and always having to be respectful to others. Kids have to know their place in the world, or the world will most likely teach them a harsh lesson.

Whenever youngsters have treated you badly—you are jostled in the street by a skateboarder, you're treated rudely by a young salesperson, or, at the extreme, your house is vandalized—you are dealing with youngsters who have not been helped to fit in and be useful.

Teenagers are naturally prone to be somewhat self-absorbed, to fit their morality to their own self-interest, and to be thought-less of others. Our job as parents is to engage them in vigorous discussions about their obligations to others, fairness, and plain right and wrong. We must reinforce some basics: "Be respon-sible. Think things through. Consider others. Think of conse-quences." Just loving your kids isn't enough; some toughness is necessary. Mothers begin this, fathers reinforce it, and elders add their weight if it still hasn't sunk in.

One good strategy is to have boys involved in service to others— to the elderly, disabled, or young children whom they help or teach. They learn the satisfaction of service and grow in self-worth at the same time.

circles are really just loose collections that offer very little sharing or emotional support.

The worst thing we can do with adolescents is leave them alone. This is why we need those really great school teachers, sports coaches, scout leaders, youth workers, and many other sources of adult involvement at this age. We need enough so that there is someone special for each kid—and that's a tall order.

Today we mostly get mothering right, and active fathering is undergoing a great resurgence. Finding good mentors for the kids in our community is the next big hurdle.

Gender Differences Are Real!

Our ideas about gender differences have changed dramatically over the years. For many centuries, biological difference was used as a reason to keep women's lives in narrow roles. The waste of talent and the frustration of life chances was horrendous. Women were not allowed to vote, get equal pay, own property, and so on. They were not supposed to join the paid workforce, or if they did, it was as a nurse, never a doctor; a secretary, never a boss. Turning this on its head—affirming that women could do anything men could—was one of the most important social movements of the twentieth century.

Then, for about thirty years, from the 1960s to the early 1990s, it was thought that boys and girls had no differences other than those that we instilled in them through conditioning— the clothes and toys we gave them, and how we treated them. Well-meaning parents and lots of preschools and schools got quite fanatical about this, working hard to get the boys to play with dolls and the girls with Lego bricks. It was felt that if we raised all children the same, gender differences and problems would disappear. But gradually the evidence mounted that there were important and immutable differences that were simply wired in. (Some were blindingly obvious; for instance, in all cultures girls enter puberty, on average, two years before boys do, which causes much havoc in the world of schoolyard romance.)

With the advent of brain-scanning technology, this argument was pretty much settled. Today, we are focused on understanding the differences and making sure they aren't a problem. If a girl's brain develops more quickly than a boy's, we can plan accordingly so teachers in schools and parents at home can manage it. If a boy has a built-in need to be active and use his body a lot more than a girl does, we can work out ways for this to happen. We can be sure to read to boys so that they become more verbal and able to talk to girls! We can have less blame and more understanding.

In the next two chapters, we will look at two major differences that are very significant in learning to help our sons grow up well:

- How hormones (such as testosterone) influence boys' behavior, and what to do about it
- How boys' and girls' brains grow differently and affect their ways of behaving and thinking

PRACTICAL HELP

Knowing the Differences

Some of the real gender differences are so obvious that it's amazing they were ever overlooked. For example, the average boy has 30 percent more muscle bulk than the average girl. Boys are stronger and their bodies are more inclined to action. They even have far more red blood cells (the original red-blooded boy!). It has nothing to do with gender conditioning. We have to give boys lots of time to exercise—girls, too. Boys require extra help to control themselves from hitting each other and girls. Girls need help to learn not to use their better verbal skills to put boys down. And so on.

This *doesn't* mean "every boy must . . ." or "every girl must . . ." After all, some girls are stronger and more physical than most boys. (Some girls need training in nonviolence. At a school in Sydney, Australia, parents removed their sons because girls kept hitting them.) Gender differences are generalizations that are true enough of the time to be very helpful.

PRACTICAL HELP

Boys and Hearing

Colin is ten. He is in trouble at school because he doesn't pay attention. He gets bored, starts to mess around, gets sent to the principal's office. Is he stupid? Bad? Does he have ADHD or ODD (Oppositional Defiant Disorder) or OCD (Obsessive-Compulsive Disorder) or any of the other Ds? Perhaps, but there's another possibility. *What if he just can't hear?* What if his teacher's voice is too soft, and he gets bored with its faintness, and at home he misses half of what is being said to him? Many parents joke that their son seems deaf when told to clean up his room. And school nurses have long noted that boys get blocked ears more frequently than girls do. But there may be more serious factors at play.

Psychologist Leonard Sax, in his book *Why Gender Matters*, makes some amazing claims about boys' hearing. He presents research to show that boys do not hear as well as girls, and argues that boys need teachers who speak louder. He cites Janel Caine, a postgraduate student in Florida, who studied the effects of music on premature babies. These babies lie in their incubators all day, and Caine felt that perhaps some gentle music might help their growth and development. And boy, was she right. In her astonishing findings, girl babies receiving music "therapy" were discharged from the hospital on average nine days sooner than those who didn't have the music. It really perked them up! But here's the thing—*boy babies did not show any such benefit.* They either didn't hear the music, or it didn't affect them.

It's actually hard to know what tiny babies hear; we can't just ask them, "Did you hear that?" But scientists recently have discovered methods that tell whether the brain is getting the message that goes into the ears. Dr. Sax claims that in studies of "acoustic brain response" girl babies have an 80 percent greater brain response to sounds than baby boys do. And guess what frequency this is in? The frequency of speech.

And the difference continues into adolescence and adulthood. This might explain that terrible syndrome teenage girls complain about worldwide—that Dad is always yelling at them, when Dad thinks he is using a gentle voice!

In a number of recent commentaries, however, Dr. Sax has been accused of exaggerating or misrepresenting the research, or making sweeping claims from fairly obscure studies. It does seem that if a huge gender hearing difference were the norm, audiologists would have told us about it by now.

Nonetheless, there is no harm in being more hearing aware around boys. And Dads, if your daughter winces when you talk to her, maybe talk a little softer.

It's also possible that the problem of boys in school is not so much to do with hearing as with understanding. Australian audiologists Jan Pollard and Dr. Kathy Rowe found that about a quarter of children aged six have poor auditory processing (separating what they hear into meaningful words). And most of these children (70 percent) turn out to be boys. These children have trouble understanding a sentence if it has more than eight words in it! Because teachers often use much longer sentences when teaching, these kids are stuck trying to understand the first part while the teacher (or parent) is going full steam ahead with the rest of the message. The researchers recommend that teachers use short sentences and only go on speaking when they see that "lights go on" effect in children's eyes. And Dr. Sax adds that perhaps boys should sit at the front of the class, not the back.

In a Nutshell

1. In the years between birth and six, boys need lots of affection so they can learn to love. Talking and teaching one-on-one helps them connect to the world. The mother is usually the best person to provide this, although the father can take this part.

2. At about the age of six, boys show a strong interest in maleness, and the father becomes the primary parent. His interest and time become critical. The mother's part remains important, however, and she shouldn't back off from her son just because he is older.

3. From about fourteen years of age, boys begin to need mentors—other adults who care about them personally and help them move gradually into the larger world. Old societies provided initiation to mark this stage, and mentors were much more available.

4. Single mothers can raise boys well but must search carefully for good, safe, male role models and must devote some time to self-care (as they are doing the work of two). Fathers in the community should reach out to and include the kids who don't have dads of their own.

5. Single dads also need to find good support networks, and must prepare to be more nurturing so they can be a safe anchor for their sons and daughters.

CHAPTER THREE

Testosterone!

Janine is pregnant—seven weeks pregnant—and very excited. She doesn't know it yet, but her baby is going to be a boy. We say "going to be," because a fetus doesn't start that way! It may surprise you to know that all young creatures start life as a female. The Y chromosome that makes a baby into a boy is an "add-on" chromosome that starts to act in the womb well into the pregnancy—to give a boy the extra parts he needs to be a boy and to stop other parts from growing. A male is a female with optional extras. That's why everyone has nipples, though not everyone needs them.

The Testosterone Cycle

In Janine's baby's tiny body, at around the eighth week of pregnancy, the Y chromosomes stir in the cells and testosterone starts being made. As a result of this new chemical presence, the baby starts to become more of a boy—growing testicles and a penis, and undergoing other more subtle changes in his brain and body. Once the testicles are formed (by the fifteenth week they are fully developed), they start to make extra testosterone, too, so he becomes progressively masculine.

If Janine is *very* stressed, perhaps as a result of a recent family grief or trauma, her body may suppress the testosterone in baby Jamie's body, and he may not fully develop his penis and testicles, and so will be incompletely developed at birth. He will catch up, however, in the first year.

Right after birth, young Jamie will have as much testosterone in his bloodstream as a twelve-year-old boy! He needs all this testosterone to stimulate his body to develop male qualities by the time he is born. This "testosterone hangover" will result in his having little erections from time to time as a newborn.

By three months of age, the testosterone level will drop off to about a fifth of the birth levels, and throughout toddlerhood the levels will stay pretty low. Boy and girl toddlers (I'm sure you'd agree) behave pretty much the same.

At the age of *four*, for reasons nobody quite understands, boys receive a sudden surge of testosterone—doubling their blood levels. At this age, little Jamie may become much more interested in action, heroics, adventures, and vigorous play. His dad may well find that this age is a good one because Jamie can now play ball games; they can do gardening together and interact in ways that were not possible when he was little and helpless.

At *five* years of age, the testosterone level drops by a half, and young Jamie calms down again, just in time for school! Enough testosterone is still around for him to be interested in activity, adventure, and exploration, but not especially interested in girls.

Somewhere between the ages of *eleven* and *thirteen*, the level starts to rise sharply again. Eventually—usually around age fourteen—it will increase by some 800 percent over the toddlerhood level. The result is a sudden growth and elongation of the boy's arms and legs—to the extent that his whole nervous system has to rewire itself. (For computer buffs, it's a little like installing the latest version of Windows!) In about 50 percent of boys, the testosterone level gets so high that some converts into estrogen, and breast swelling and tenderness may be experienced. This is nothing to worry about.

Brains Go out the Window

Around age *thirteen*, the reorganization of Jamie's brain, linked with the rapid growth of his body, makes him dopey and disorganized for many months. His mother and father have to act as his substitute brain for a while! If they're not aware of the reasons for this, parents can wonder where they have gone wrong. If Jamie's parents know this is all part of puberty and take a relaxed, but vigilant attitude, things should work out just fine.

By age *fourteen*, the testosterone level is at a peak, and pubic hair, acne, strong sexual feelings, and general restlessness may well drive Jamie and everyone around him slightly crazy. For most families, this is the most challenging year of raising boys. Take comfort: if you hang in there and stay caring and firm, it does pass. In the later teens, boys become increasingly more sensible and mature.

When Jamie reaches his *mid-twenties*, things settle down, hormonally speaking. His testosterone level is just as high, but his body has become used to this and he is not quite so reactive. Erections are a little more under control! The hormone continues to endow him with male features—such as high cholesterol, baldness, hairy nostrils, and so on—well into later life. On the plus side, the testosterone gives him surges of creative energy, a love of competition, and a desire to achieve and to be protective. Ideally, his energies will be channeled into activities and career choices (as well as a happy sex life) that bring all kinds of satisfaction and benefits.

In his early *forties*, Jamie's levels of testosterone begin a very gradual decline. He goes for several days at a time without thinking about sex! In the bedroom, quality replaces quantity. In the world, Jamie now has less to prove and is more mellow and wise. He assumes quiet leadership in group and work situations, rather than having to prove who's boss. He values friendship and makes his best contributions to the world.

EACH BOY IS UNIQUE

What we have described here is the pattern for the average boy. There is wide variation among males and also lots of overlap between the sexes. Some girls will have more testosterone-type behavior than some boys, and some boys will show more estrogen-type behavior than some girls. Nonetheless, the general pattern will hold true for most children.

Understanding boys' hormones and their effects means we can understand what is going on and be sympathetic and helpful. Just as a good husband understands if his partner has PMS (premenstrual syndrome), a good parent of a boy understands his TNT (testosterone needing tutoring).

Why Boys Scuffle and Fight

Testosterone also affects mood and energy—it is more than just a growth hormone. There's no doubt it causes energetic and boisterous behavior. That's why, for centuries, horses have been gelded to make them better behaved. Female rats injected with testosterone try to mate with other female rats and fight with each other. It makes certain parts of the brain grow and others slow down in growth. It can grow more muscles and less fat, and it can make you go bald and bad-tempered!

A famous study illustrates how testosterone affects the psychology of males. A tribe of monkeys in a laboratory was

PRACTICAL HELP

Teenage Boys and Driving

The biggest single worry all parents of boys share is about safety. In the adolescent years especially, as they spend more time away from your direct care, and their mobility and independence grows, it's hard to relax and just let go. And in fact there is growing evidence that this fear is well grounded—that we are letting go too soon. This is especially true in the matter of driving cars. Every year, in every industrialized nation, the newspapers carry stories of small towns or suburban communities devastated by multiple fatality crashes, in which four or five teenagers die in a collision caused by immaturity and inexperience.

As a community, we care deeply about the lives of our young people, and this has prompted some astoundingly clear research into why boys die like this and how to prevent it. The first finding is that *one* boy in his late teens, on his own driving a car, is relatively safe. Today's emphasis on driver training and fifty to a hundred hours of practice driving with an adult supervising them (usually Mom or Dad) means boys have greater awareness and skill than young drivers did back when we were teenagers. They probably drive too fast at times, but they are also more focused and attentive to driving, so they do not fare too badly as long as alcohol is not involved. However, if you add another male passenger in the car, things begin to change: the chances of a fatal crash increase by 50 percent. Something changes in the attitude of the young driver. He takes more risks. If the passenger is a girl, however, he becomes protective and careful, and is actually safer than on his own.

The next fact may shock you. If you add one or more other young people in the backseat, the death risk of the driver increases *by over 400 percent*. The distraction; the need to impress; the difficulty of staying in a calm, careful state of mind all mean that all those in the car are at serious risk. This is especially so after dark, and of course is much worse with drugs or alcohol present. This research has led to law reforms that are saving lives around the world. In Australia, bereaved father Rob Wells has single-handedly persuaded governments in several states to restrict young drivers from carrying more than one passenger, especially late at night. These laws have worked very effectively in New Zealand and Canada for many years. Rob and I are convinced these laws do not go far enough; first-year drivers probably should have a passenger limit of one at all times.

At the time of this writing, thirty-one U.S. and Canadian jurisdictions have some form of graduated licensing for young drivers. Florida led the way, but it's Ontario in Canada that has the best record—a combination of graduated stages of licensing and restrictions on passenger numbers has reduced deaths of young drivers by 30 percent.

Meanwhile, it helps that parents know and can make their own decisions. Sixteen-year-olds are too young to drive groups of friends around at any time. You have ferried them around for fifteen years already—why not do it for one more year or two, to make sure they won't die or kill their friends?

At sixteen, teenagers can sound persuasive. They can say the right things. But it's later, under pressure, that their brains are not able to cope. The last thing parents of dead teenagers ever hear them say is "I'll be fine, Mom." If they wait a year or two, and gain more experience with daytime driving, they will be so much safer.

closely observed to learn about its social structure. Researchers found that the male monkeys had a definite hierarchy, or pecking order. The females' hierarchy was looser and more relaxed, and based on who groomed whose hair! But the males always knew who was boss, and sub-boss, and sub-sub-boss, and had frequent fights to prove it.

Once the researchers had worked out the monkey dynamics, they set about to stir up trouble. They captured the lowest-ranking male monkey and gave him an injection of testosterone. Then they put him back with the tribe. You can guess what happened next. He started a boxing match with his "immediate superior." Much to his own surprise, he won! So he went and took on the next monkey! Within twenty minutes he had worked his way up and tossed off the biggest monkey from the highest branch. Our hero was small, but he had *testosterone*! He became the "acting manager."

Sadly for him, this was not to last. The injection soon wore off, and our little conqueror was knocked back all the way down to the bottom of the heap. It's a lot like politics! The point is that testosterone influences the brain and makes boys more concerned with rank and competition.

Boys Need Order

In their book, *Raising a Son*, Don and Jeanne Elium tell the story of an old scoutmaster who comes and sorts out a hopelessly rowdy scout troop in their city. This is the "scout troop from hell": the boys are always fighting and damaging the hall, nothing is being learned, and many gentler boys have left the troop. It's time for a clean sweep. On his first night with the troop, the scoutmaster sets some rules, invites a couple of boys to shape up or leave, brings in a clear structure, and begins teaching skills in an organized way. He successfully turns the group around. In a couple of months it is thriving.

The scoutmaster explained to the Eliums that in his experience there are three things boys always need to know:

1. Who's in charge?
2. What are the rules?
3. Will those rules be fairly enforced?

THE KEY WORD IS STRUCTURE

Boys feel insecure and in danger if there isn't enough structure in a situation. If no one is in charge, they begin jostling with each other to establish the pecking order. Their testosterone-driven makeup leads them to want to set up hierarchies, but they can't always do it because they are all the same age. If we provide structure, they can relax. For girls, this is not so much of a problem.

Many years ago I spent time in the slums of Calcutta to learn about families there. At first glance, Calcutta seemed chaotic and frightening. In fact, there were gang lords and neighborhood hierarchies, and these, for better or worse, provided a structure for people to live their lives. They were safer with some structure—even a mafia-like structure—than with none. As a better structure was provided, by religious or community leaders who were trustworthy and competent, life got even better. Wherever you see a gang of boys looking unruly, you know the adult leadership is failing. Boys form gangs for survival. It's their attempt to have a sense of belonging, order, and safety.

Boys act tough to cover up their fear. If someone is clearly the boss, they relax. But the boss must not be erratic or punitive. If the person in charge is a bully, the boys' stress levels rise, and it's back to the law of the jungle. If the teacher, scoutmaster, or parent is kind and fair (as well as strict), boys will drop their macho act and get on with learning.

This seems to be a built-in gender difference. If girls are anxious in a group setting, they tend to cower and be quiet, whereas boys respond by running around, making a lot of noise. This has been seen as boys "dominating the space." However, it is actually an anxiety response. Schools that are very good at engaging boys in interesting and concrete activities (such as Montessori schools, which stress a lot of structural work with blocks, shapes, beads, and so on) do not experience this gender difference in children's behavior.

Not everyone accepts that hormones affect boys' behavior. Some feminist biologists have argued that men have testosterone through conditioning—that it comes from being raised that way. There is actually a partial truth in this. One study found that boys in scary or violent school environments produced more testosterone. When the same school introduced a more supportive environment (where teachers did not abuse or threaten, and bullying was tackled with special programs), the boys' levels of testosterone dropped measurably. So environment *and* biology both play a part.

But environment only *influences* the hormone. Nature—and boys' built-in calendar—creates it. Success with boys means accepting their nature while directing it in good ways. If you know what you are dealing with, it's a whole lot easier, and you don't need to blame anyone—just help them find a better way.

How Did Male and Female Differences Come About?

Evolution is constantly changing the shape of all living creatures. For instance, early humans had huge jaws and teeth for chewing raw food. But when they discovered fires and cooking, over many generations their jaws and teeth became smaller because food was softer to chew. If we have a few thousand years of eating fast food we may end up chinless altogether!

Some gender differences are obvious in human beings—size, hairiness, and so on. But the main differences are the hidden ones. These came about through taking very different roles for a very large part of our history. Hunter-gatherer societies divided the work very much along gender lines. For 99 percent of human history, the women mostly gathered, and the men mostly hunted.

Hunting was a specialized activity. It required quick team action with sudden and strong muscular activity in short bursts, and you had to be very single-minded. Once the chase was on, there was no time for discussion. Someone was in charge, and you did what you were told or got eaten or gored by a large animal.

The women's work of gathering seeds, roots, and insects was different. It allowed time for discussion, required finger dexterity and sensitivity, and included the care of babies and children. As a result, all human females have finger sensitivity several times greater than males. The women's work required caution, constancy, and attention to detail—whereas hunting required a certain degree of recklessness or even

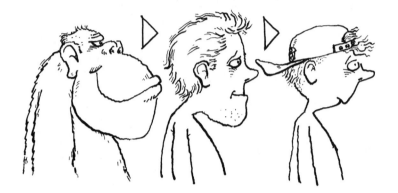

EVOLUTION OF THE HUMAN JAW

self-sacrifice. Women's bodies became generally smaller but better able to persist and endure. Men's bodies were better at rapid bursts of strength but more likely to be laid low by a case of the flu or an ingrown toenail! The differences were not great, and some role flexibility probably helped. So we ended up a species with slight but significant differences between male and female bodies and brains.

The Links Between Sex and Aggression

There is some support from primate studies for the idea that males with more power have higher sex drives. Men on sports teams that win have a higher testosterone level (after the game) than those who lose. And according to historians, many great leaders (President Kennedy, for instance) had a very high sex drive, to a degree that was really rather tragic and disabling. (It's kind of hard to run a country when you want to keep sneaking off to have sex all the time.)

One study of juvenile delinquency in the 1980s found an intriguing connection—that boys were several times more likely to get into trouble with the police in the six months before their first sexual experience. In other words, they calmed down a bit once they started having sex. Since almost all boys masturbate at this age, it can't have been just the release of sexual frustration. Perhaps the boys felt they had "joined the human race" when they found a real-life lover. Perhaps they felt more loved.

Sex and aggression are somewhat linked—controlled by the same centers in the brain and by the same hormone group. This has been the source of enormous human tragedy and suffering, inflicted in sexual assaults on women, children, and men. Because of this connection, it is very important that boys are helped to relate to women as people, to have empathy, and to learn to be good lovers.

It's never an excuse for male aggression to blame hormones. But it's vital that we separate the stimuli of violence from the stimuli of sex. We shouldn't really make or show movies that link the two. The rape-revenge plot of many B-grade movies is a bad connection to make. Most pornography is in fact pretty dismal role-modeling for good relating or sensitive and joyous loving. Where are the movie depictions of tender, sensuous, playful, and boisterous lovemaking (with plots that include conversation, sharing, and vulnerability), so that mid-adolescent boys can learn a fuller kind of sexuality?

Overcoming sexual violence may just come down to treating children more kindly. Raymond Wyre, a British expert on working with men who sexually abuse children, found in his work that although not every sex offender had been the victim of sexual assault (though many had been), every one, without exception, had been the recipient of a very cruel and uncaring childhood. He felt that the lack of empathy, resulting from never having been shown consistent understanding and kindness, was the key factor determining whether someone will sexually assault another human being.

Guiding the "High Drive" Boys

Testosterone provides energy and focus. A boy with high levels of the hormone makes good leadership material. Early in the school year, teachers often notice a certain kind of boy who will become either a hero of the class or a complete villain. For this boy there is no middle ground. This type of boy exhibits three distinctive marker behaviors:

- Challenging behavior and competitiveness
- Greater physical maturity
- High energy levels

If the teacher is able to befriend such a boy and direct his energies in good ways, the boy will thrive and be a plus in the school. If a teacher or parent ignores, backs off, or is negative toward the boy, the boy's pride will depend on defeating the adult and problems will compound. These boys have leadership potential, but leadership has to be taught from an early age.

In a Nutshell

Testosterone in varying degrees affects every boy.

1. It gives him growth spurts, makes him want to be active, and makes him competitive and in need of strong guidelines and a safe, ordered environment.

2. It triggers significant changes:
   - At four—activity and boyishness
   - At thirteen—rapid growth and disorientation
   - At fourteen—testing limits and breaking through to early manhood

3. The boy with testosterone in his bloodstream likes to know who is the boss but also must be treated fairly. Bad environments bring out the worst in him. The boy with lots of testosterone needs special help to develop leadership qualities and channel his energies in good ways.

4. A boy needs to learn empathy and feeling and be shown tenderness if he is to be a sexually caring being.

5. Some girls have a lot of testosterone but, on the whole, it's a boy thing—and needs our understanding, not blame or ridicule. Testosterone equals vitality, and it's our job to honor it and steer it in healthy directions.

CHAPTER FOUR

How Boys' and Girls' Brains Differ

The brain of a baby in the womb grows very rapidly, developing in a month or two from just a few cells into one of the most complex structures in nature. By the sixth month of pregnancy a fetus has impressive abilities, all controlled by its brain—such as recognizing your voice, responding to movements, even kicking back when prodded! With ultrasound, you can actually see it moving its mouth as if it is singing in the womb.

At birth the brain is still only partially formed—and only a third of its eventual size. It takes a long time for the brain to be completed. For instance, the language part of the brain is not fully formed until about the age of thirteen. (This is why it is so important that boys are kept up with reading through the primary school years.)

From very early on, gender differences are evident in the unborn baby's brain. One difference is that a baby boy's brain develops more slowly than a baby girl's. Another difference is that the left and right sides are less well connected in a boy.

All animal brains have two halves. In simple animals (like lizards or birds) this means that everything is duplicated. A bang on the head might wipe out part of one half of the brain, but the other half can take care of things. However, in humans (who have a lot more to think about!), the two brain halves specialize somewhat. One half handles language and reasoning; the other handles movement, emotion, and the senses of space and position. Both halves talk to each other through a big central bundle of fibers called the corpus callosum (which sounds like the name of a Catholic school). The corpus callosum in boys is proportionately smaller in size—there are fewer connections running from one side to the other.

It has been shown in recent studies that boys tend to attack certain kinds of problems (such as a spelling quiz or word puzzle) using only one side of their brain, while girls use *both* sides. This can be vividly seen using the brain-scanning technology of magnetic resonance imaging (MRI). The "lights go on" all over a girl's brain, while in a boy they tend to be localized on

one part of one side only. This has enormous ramifications (examined later on).

Why the difference?

The brain of a baby before and after birth grows rather like a jar of alfalfa sprouts accidentally left in the sun—brain cells keep getting longer and making new connections all the time. The left half of the cortex grows more slowly than the right in all human babies, but in males it is even slower still. The testosterone in a boy's bloodstream slows things down. Estrogen, the hormone that is predominant in the bloodstream of baby girls, actually stimulates faster growth of brain cells.

As the right half grows, it tries to make connections with the left half of the brain. In boys, the left half is not yet ready to take the connections, and so the nerve cells reaching across from the right cannot find a place to "plug in." So they go back to the right side where they came from and plug in there instead. As a result, the right half in a boy's brain is richer in internal connections but poorer in cross connections to the other half. This is one possible explanation of boys' greater success in mathematics (which is largely a "right-brain" activity) and their greater interest in taking machinery to pieces and leaving the bits lying around! But we must be careful not to give these conclusions too much weight, as sometimes parental expectations, practice, and social pressure also influence skills and abilities. It's clear that practice actually helps more brain connections lay down permanently, so encouragement and teaching actually affect the shape and power of the brain in later life.

Whether the cause is hormonal or environmental, there is no doubt that these brain differences exist between men and women today. Because of their more connected brain halves, older women who suffer strokes usually recover more speedily and completely than men. They can activate extra pathways to the other half of their brain to do the job of the damaged parts. Girls who have learning problems improve more quickly with tutoring for the same reason. And boys are more prone to problems resulting from brain damage at birth. This may explain the greater numbers of boys with learning difficulties, autism, and many other brain-related disorders.

Brain scanning has found a total of seven structural differences between boys' and girls' brains, though these are still poorly understood.

Why Is It Important to Know about Brains?

Knowing about the differences in boys' brains helps explain some practical difficulties that boys have, and what to do about them.

If your brain is somewhat less connected from right to left, you will have trouble doing things well that need both sides of the brain. This involves skills such as *reading, talking about feelings*, and solving problems through *quiet introspection* rather than by beating people over the head! Do these problems sound at all familiar to you? Now you can see the importance of all this brain research!

PRACTICAL HELP

Learning to Communicate

Communication is essential to life. Yet sadly, in every classroom, there are about four or five children who can't read, write, or speak well. And among these children boys outnumber girls by four to one! This is now thought to be the result of boys' brains not being quite so well organized for language.

But there is no need to just let this be. If you want to help your child avoid learning or language problems, there is a lot you can do, according to neuroscientist Dr. Jenny Harasty. Dr. Harasty and her team found that in females, two regions of the brain dedicated to handling language are proportionately 20 to 30 percent larger than in males. But no one knows whether these regions are larger at birth, or larger because girls get more practice at using them, causing them to grow. Whatever the cause, we do know that the brain is very responsive to learning experiences if these are given at the right age. And for language, that age is birth to thirteen, although the earlier years, birth to eight, are the

most critical. In adolescence and adulthood we go on learning, but the older the child, the harder it is to change that early wiring of the brain.

You can help your boy learn to communicate better, starting right from when he is a baby. This means that he will be a better reader, writer, and speaker when he goes to school. Here's how:

1. "TALK THEM UP"—ONE STEP AT A TIME

Children acquire spoken language one step at a time. Babies under one year of age will begin to babble and gesture very enthusiastically, telling us they are ready to learn verbal communication! This is the time to help them learn words.

With a baby who babbles, repeat a word that seems to be what they mean. Baby says "gukuk, baguk!" and points to his toy duck. You say "Ducky! John's ducky!" Soon John will be saying "Ducky" too.

With a toddler who says single words, like "milk," you say a couple of words, such as "milk bottle." This helps him move on to joining pairs of words together, and so on.

A child who is saying words in twos and threes can be stretched further by imitating you in whole sentences. For example, he says "Gavin truck!" You reply, "Gavin wants a truck? Here's Gavin's truck!" And so on.

In short, kids learn best if you speak back to them one step ahead of the stage they are at. And they love the game. All human beings love to communicate.

2. EXPLAIN THINGS TO CHILDREN EVERY CHANCE YOU CAN

This is a great use of the many times when you are just doing routine things with your children—traveling, doing housework, going for a walk, doing the shopping. Use this time to chatter, point things out, answer questions. Surprisingly, some very loving parents (who care for their kids well) seem not to realize that kids' brains grow from conversation. Don't be shy—explain things, tell them stories! For example, "You see this lever? This makes the wipers go. They swish the rain away from the window." "This vacuum cleaner makes a big wind. It sucks the air and pulls the dirt into a bag. Would you like a turn?"

This kind of talk—provided you don't overdo it and bore your child to tears—does more for your child's brain than any amount of expensive education later on.

3. READ TO YOUR KIDS FROM AN EARLY AGE

Even when your child is just one year old, you can enjoy books together—especially the kind that have rhymes and repetition. "Humpty Dumpty" and "Twinkle Twinkle Little Star" work just fine. From enjoying books at your knee, or snuggled up in bed, children learn to love the reading experience, looking at the pictures and enjoying the sound of your voice. You can ham it up a little by making funny voices or being dramatic.

As your child gets to have favorite stories, you can play a "predicting" game—"And the little cat went . . . ?" pausing so your child provides the "meow!" Prediction is a very important part of reading. Good readers anticipate what word is coming next.

Remember, whenever playing learning games with kids, the trick is to be playful, making your children stretch their minds just a little—which they will love to do.

All kids benefit from these three learning practices—but for boys it is a preventive step because of their disposition to be poorer at language if we don't help them along. And it's fun to do, anyway!

Dr. Jenny Harasty advises that if you have worries about your boy's speech and language development (if he isn't talking as well as you think he should), trust your intuition. Speak to a speech pathologist from your local hospital or community health center. Sessions of speech therapy can be fun for children and can make all the difference to a good start.

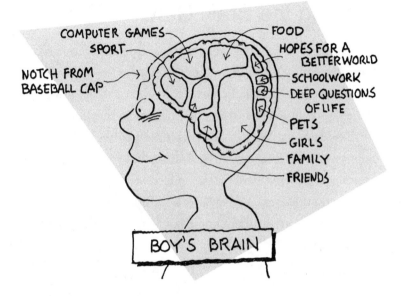

Danger: Sexism Alert!

There is a vitally important point to be made here. To say that "boys are different" can very easily turn into an excuse for saying "they are defective" or, worse still, "they can't help it." The same sort of generalizations were once applied to girls: "They'll never be any good at science or engineering." "They're too emotional to be in responsible jobs," and so on. So please take the following points very seriously:

- The differences are slight for most people.
- They are only tendencies.
- They don't apply to every individual.
- Most important of all, we can help boys overcome any negative tendencies that stem from brain differences.

Helping the Brain Grow

We can work to help boys read better, express themselves better, solve conflicts better, and empathize better—and so help them to be great human beings. Schools have equity programs to help girls in mathematics and sciences so they have access to these careers. We are now beginning to see that we can help boys with language arts, drama, and so on, which can better equip them to live in the modern world. (For some great ways to do this, see chapter 8, "A Revolution in Schooling.")

Our brains are brilliant and flexible devices, always able to learn. A parent can help a boy learn skills like these:

- How to figure out people's feelings from the expressions on their faces
- How to make friends and join in a game or conversation
- How to read his own body signals—for example, to know when he is getting angry and needs to walk away from a situation

By working on these skills with their sons, parents are building connections from one side of their son's brain to the other.

In school the same help is needed. One young math teacher I know rarely lets a lesson pass without using some hands-on example of what was being studied—often going outside to do it in a practical way in the school yard. She has found that the less motivated of her students can get a grasp of the concepts if they see them in practice and do physical things with their bodies to comprehend the idea being taught. They are getting right-brain concepts to link to their left-brain understanding—using their strengths to overcome their weaknesses. This teacher's boy students love learning from her; she is adventurous and keen, and truly cares about them.

Boys Are Not Inferior— Just Different

Having a well-developed right side of the brain, as boys tend to do, has many pluses. As well as having mathematical and mechanical abilities, males tend to be action-oriented—if they see a problem, they want to fix it. The right side of the brain handles both feelings and actions, so men are more likely to take action, whereas women tend to mull things over! It requires extra effort for a boy to shift into his left hemisphere and find the words to explain the feelings he is registering in his right hemisphere. But when he does, he is often poignantly honest and open.

About twice a month I meet with the staff of different schools to teach about boys' education. At one point I always ask for some volunteers to talk about why they like teaching boys. It's a lovely and touching moment to hear female teachers talk about how boys are honest, upfront about what they think and feel, and forgiving, soon getting over a hurt or confrontation, whereas girls who decide they don't like someone can stay that way for weeks! These teachers are the ones who do well with boys and look forward to teaching them; they like the challenge, the energy, the way it brings out the best in them as teachers, and the fact that they can make a difference in a boy's life. The research backs this up—boys only learn well if they sense that the teacher actually likes them as

PRACTICAL HELP

Starting School: Why Boys Should Start Later

Boys' brain differences have one huge implication—that of decid-ing when boys should start school. I have talked now to tens of thousands of parents, many of whom have taken this on board and found great benefits for their boys. If you have a son who has not started school yet, read this next section carefully—it could make a huge difference in his life.

At the age of five or six, when children start serious schooling, boys' brains are an astonishing six to twelve months less devel-oped than girls' are. They are especially delayed in what is called *fine-motor coordination*—the ability to use their fingers carefully and hold a pen or scissors. And because they are still in the stage of gross-motor development, they will be itching to move their large muscles around—so they will not be good at sitting still.

Boys' other delay is in using words well—that is, being able to tell a teacher what they need and to communicate verbally with other children. Many boys at five are still very young socially; in fact, they are not really ready for the demands of a school environment. When I've talked to heads of primary departments (from country schools in outback Australia to big international schools in Asia and Europe), the same message comes through: "Many if not most boys would have a better school life if they could start school a year later than girls."

The calendar is actually a terrible basis for deciding who should start school; kids vary so much, and of course with a yearly intake, some will always be young for their year. (In many cases, *too* young.)

Knowing When to Start

It's clear that all children should attend kindergarten or half-day preschool, from around four years of age, as they need the social stimulation and wider experiences this provides (and because parents need a break!).

In preschool or kindergarten, it will be very clear which boys are ready for school—happy to sit and do work in books or with crafts, able to talk happily. And it will be clear which boys are still needing to run around and are not yet good with a crayon or pencil. Most boys of ages four to five will fall into the second group.

Based on your own observation, discussion with the preschool teacher, and perhaps checking out what is expected of children going into primary school, you will soon get an idea—he's ready, or he's not ready yet. By taking another year in preschool, your boy has a whole additional year to get ready to do really well in primary school. For most, this would mean that they move through school being more or less *a year older than the girl at the next desk*. Which also means that they are, intellectually speaking, on par with her. Eventually boys catch up with girls intellectually but, in the way schools work now, the damage is already done. Many boys feel themselves to be failures for this reason; they miss out on key skills because they are just not ready and so get turned off from learning. To emphasize again, this is not a hard and fast rule: some boys are perfectly ready to start school at five and do just fine. The key point is taking each child individually on readiness, not just on age.

It helps if school is made more boy-friendly in any case. Sitting still at a desk for a long time is usually hard and painful for boys (and some girls, too). In early primary school, boys (whose motor nerves are still growing) actually get signals from their body saying, "Move around. Use me." To a stressed-out first grade teacher, this looks like misbehavior. A boy sees that his craft work, drawing, and writing are not as good as the girls' and thinks, "This is not for me!" He quickly switches off from learning—especially if there are no male teachers anywhere in the school. "School is for girls," he tells himself.

There is much more that we can do to make school good for boys. This is explored in chapter 8. But the question we began with—is he ready yet?—is perhaps the most important.

a person. I guess this applies to a boy's relationship with his parents, too. When they know we love them, that's the foundation of being able to guide them and help them grow.

A New Kind of Man

The world no longer needs men who can hunt buffalo or cut down trees with a flint ax. In the modern world, in which manual or mechanical labor is less and less needed, we need to take that masculine ability and energy and redirect it to a different kind of heroic effort. This means adding language and feeling skills to the thinking and doing skills of boys—making a kind of "superboy" who is flexible across all kinds of skill areas.

If you think about it, the great men throughout history—Gandhi, Martin Luther King Jr., Buddha, Jesus—actually were like this. They had courage and determination, along with sensitivity and love for others. It's an unbeatable mix, and it is certainly needed today.

In a Nutshell

The gender differences male hormones and male genes create need to be handled in practical ways. The next two pages sum up what you can do with your boy to help him be a "new kind of man."

PRACTICAL HELP

What Boys Need

Because Boys Often:	We Need To:
. . . are prone to separation anxiety . . .	. . . show them as much affection as we do girls, and avoid separations, such as leaving them in daycare before the age of three.
. . . have testosterone surges making them sometimes argumentative and restless—especially around age fourteen . . .	. . . calmly guide them through conflicts—settle them down with reasoning, not with loud words or an attack. Be clear that they need to show good manners always and never use violence or even threaten anyone with violence. Fathers need to be role models and insist that mothers are respected.
. . . have growth spurts that make them vague and disorganized, especially at age thirteen (this applies to girls, too) . . .	. . . get involved in organizing them; teach them systems for tidying rooms, doing housework, tackling school projects in small bites, and having a routine.
. . . have bursts of physical energy that need to be expressed . . .	. . . be sure to have lots of space and time for exercise and moving about.
. . . have a slower rate of brain development, affecting fine motor skills in the early primary years . . .	. . . delay starting them in first grade until they have lots of pen-and-paper skills, can handle scissors, and so on.

PRACTICAL HELP *(CONTINUED)*

Because Boys Often:	We Need To:
. . . have fewer connections from the language half to the sensory half of the brain . . .	. . . read to them, tell them stories, and explain things, especially from ages one to eight.
. . . need a clear set of rules and need to know who is in charge . . .	. . . have calm, orderly environments at home and school. Avoid schools where bullying is common and kids are not well supervised.
. . . have a more muscular body . . .	. . . specifically teach them not to hit or hurt others; also, teach them to use words to communicate. (See my book *Complete Secrets of Happy Children* for ways to discipline that don't involve hitting, shaming, or blaming.)
. . . have a tendency to act first without thinking of the consequences . . .	. . . talk with them often in a friendly way about options, choices, ways to solve problems, and what they can do in situations in their lives.

CHAPTER FIVE

What Dads Can Do

My daughter is now a young woman, but it only seems like yesterday that she was born. That was a day to remember! We had planned on a home birth, but also allowed for a hospital transfer if necessary. And sure enough, the labor ended with an emergency caesarean at about 3 A.M.—not at all what we had hoped for. The pact I'd made with my wife Shaaron was, nobody else takes this baby. So I was there in the operating room, and our baby went straight from the weighing scales and into my arms. While Shaaron recovered from the operation over the next few days, I slept on a stretcher bed on the floor of her hospital room, our baby tucked beside me—which caused shrieks of shock from several new shift nurses when they stumbled in for the 2 A.M. shift change. It was a great system—Shaaron knew the baby was close and safe, not off in a nursery somewhere, and I could hand her up to her mom for breastfeeding at any time. Sometimes a nurse would discreetly take Shaaron aside and ask if this was what she really wanted. She would smile and say, "Yes, of course!"

Fighting to Be a Dad

The experience of my daughter's birth showed in a way what it is like to be a dad these days—you have to make a firm stand, sometimes even fight, to be allowed to *be* a dad. The world doesn't seem to want you to be an involved parent. They'd rather have you stay late at the office. Someone else will teach your children to hit a ball, play piano, and believe in themselves. You just pay the bills.

Luckily, fathers are fighting their way back into family life, and they are very welcome, too. Twentieth-century fathering was something of a disaster. Our fathers' generation included a few great dads, but most men of previous generations proved their love by working at a job far from home, not by playing, cuddling, talking, or teaching—the things kids really love. In every neighborhood some dads were violent or scary, or drank too much. Many were traumatized by war and were hard to get close to. Some men simply walked out on their families and never came back. So when we come to fathering our own children, it can feel strange—we may have little knowledge of what good fathering looks like. All we have are a few pieces of a larger jigsaw puzzle.

Things are looking up. We know from studies conducted across the developed world that fathers have increased the time they spend with children by 300 percent since the 1970s. Young dads today are determined to spend more time, and most of them succeed. In fact, with fatherhood, you never fail, as long as you don't quit. As long as you are willing to give it a try you will always achieve something. Don't be tempted to leave all the parenting to your partner. As we'll see in this chapter, men bring different things to parenting, things that

are unique and irreplaceable. The more you do, the more you will rediscover your talents at fathering and your own unique style. There is nothing as satisfying as raising great kids.

Reviving a Lost Art

A lot of fathering of boys is simple. Here are some clues:

- Most boys love to be physically active, to have fun with their fathers. They love to hug their dad and play-wrestle with him. (If they don't like it, you're probably being too rough!)
- They like to accompany you on adventures and experiences in the big, wide world—all the while feeling secure

because Dad seems so huge and capable (even if he doesn't feel that way himself half of the time).

- They love to hear stories about your life, meet your friends, and see what you do for a living.
- They love you to teach them things—anything, really. If you don't know things like fishing or making stuff in sheds or fixing go-carts or computers and so on, well, you can learn together. It's trying that counts.

Kids Learn Your Attitudes

Kids don't just learn from what you say to them; they take on your attitudes as well. A friend of mine, a Vietnam veteran, was driving with his children and pulled up at some traffic lights. An Asian family was among those crossing at the lights. My friend's four-year-old, strapped into his booster seat in the back, suddenly made a racist comment! (I won't quote it here.) But my friend recognized his own words. He was shocked to hear it from a child. It sounded ugly and wrong to him. He found a parking spot and pulled over. He told his child he was sorry that he had ever spoken like that, and he didn't want the child ever to speak like that either.

Kids Learn to Love by Watching You

Children even learn about love by watching you. They love it when you show warmth to their mother, give her a compliment, flirt, exchange a cuddle or a kiss. Most small children

PRACTICAL HELP

Mirror Neurons

In 2006 an incredible discovery was made—the existence in the body of *mirror neurons*. These are a network of nerve cells, running alongside our motor nerves, that have a unique role: they mirror, or imitate, everything we watch. So if we watch ballet, or football, or two people engaged in a passionate kiss, our mirror neurons practice this action. The mirror actions are stored in our brain, ready to make it easier to copy what we've seen. (So every couch potato really does have an inner athlete, or rock star, or red-hot lover on the inside trying to get out!) This, we now know, is the reason that we can learn skills as fast as we do. But it's a two-edged sword, because it means *everything kids see, they take into their brains and are inclined to repeat*. The ramifications of this are huge.

This certainly has implications for what we allow children to watch on TV and computer games, and the importance of not depicting violence or violent sex in the media. But it especially impacts how we behave around our kids. If children see us always grumpy, self-pitying, sneaky, lying and cheating, vicious, or mean, they become that. They take in not only our actions, but also our moods and outlook. Many a man has been horrified to notice he has the same gestures, movements, or expressions that his father used to have. Or they come out with words or sayings that their old man used to use. This is not genetic; it's "mirror learning." It's a good reason to really work on how you act around your kids.

GRANDMA!

WHERE'S THE OLD BAG?

cannot resist squeezing in whenever they see their parents hugging. They love to soak in the feeling of the two of you. When you are private, and close the bedroom door, children even learn from this some of the awe and mystery of love.

Being respectful to their mother is important. So is being self-respecting—not getting into abusive or nasty arguments. Your son needs to see not only that women are never abused, but also that a man can argue calmly, without fighting or lashing out—that he can listen but also make his point and insist on being heard.

Kids Learn to Feel by Watching You

Sons learn how to express their feelings by watching their fathers and other men. They need to see you showing all four of the basic feelings:

sadness	when someone has died or a disappointment has come along;
anger	when something has been unjust or wrong;
happiness	when things go well; and
fear	when there is danger.

Dads need to show real care in expressing feelings around their children. Dads and moms are the pillars of a child's world; the child doesn't want to see those pillars come tumbling down. So even though children need to know and see when we are angry, scared, happy, or sad, they want to know that we can "hold" those feelings. This means that we can be afraid, but not rattled; mad, but not dangerous; happy, but not stupid; and sad, but not overwhelmed or dismayed. They don't want to see us losing our grip. But they are touched and helped if we can shed a tear or honestly express anger or fear, because they have those emotions themselves all the time.

Often when men have an uncomfortable feeling they will convert it to something more comfortable. Usually anger is the most comfortable feeling for men. When a little boy has gotten lost in the shopping center or a teenager has taken a foolish risk, the father who can say, "I was scared" has much more impact than the one who yells and slams doors. If men act angry when they are really sad, scared, or even happy, this can be pretty confusing for kids.

Boys are trying to match their inner sensations with outer ways of behaving; they need us to show them how this is done.

Whatever Happens in Your Marriage, Don't Divorce Your Kids

Divorce is a huge blow to a father's hopes and dreams for his children. Some men feel so grief-stricken that they cut and run. Others have to fight the system to stay in contact with their children. It's vitally important—whatever happens to your marriage—that you stay in your children's lives. More and more fathers are sharing parenting equally (or even more so) after divorce. I've talked to men who, after divorce, decided it would be simpler for the children if they didn't maintain contact. They always profoundly regretted this decision.

Some great organizations for separated dads have sprung up; they are mostly constructive and very helpful. Also, divorce courts are now more aware that kids need fathers in their lives, and most will work to make sure that contact is shared and maintained.

For your children's sake, if your marriage comes to an end, learn to be polite and kind to your ex-partner, even if you don't always feel that way. Better still, work to preserve your partnership by giving that some time and attention too, before it's too late.

Rough-and-Tumble Games: What's Really Going On?

There's a unique father behavior that has been observed all over the world. Dads (along with big brothers, uncles, and grandpas) love to wrestle and play rough-and-tumble games with little boys. They can hardly resist it. The men and the big boys get the little boys and throw them about. The little boys come running back and say, "Do it again!"

Sydney, Australia, counselor Paul Whyte puts it very plainly: "If you want to get along with boys, learn to wrestle!"

For a long time nobody understood why this was so—especially mothers, who are usually trying to calm things down while dads seem likely to stir them up all over again! But it's been found that what boys are learning in rough-and-tumble is an essential lesson for all males: how to be able to have fun, get noisy, even get angry and, at the same time, *know when to stop.* For a male living with testosterone, this is vital. If you live in a male body, you have to learn how to drive it.

THE BIG MALE LESSON:
KNOWING WHEN TO STOP

If you've ever wrestled with a little boy—say, a three- or four-year-old—it always starts out happily enough. But often, after a minute or two, he "loses it." He gets angry. His little jaw starts to jut! He knits his eyebrows together and (if you haven't spotted the warning signs yet) starts to get serious and hit out with knees and elbows. Ouch!

A dad who knows what he's doing stops the action right there. *"Hoooooold it! Stop!"* Then a little lecture takes place—not yelling, just calmly explaining.

"Your body is precious [pointing at boy], and my body is precious, too. We can't play this game if somebody might get hurt. So we need a few rules—like, *No elbowing* and *no kneeing or punching!* Do you understand? Can you handle it?" (Here's a tip: always say "Can you handle it?" rather than "Will you keep the rules?" which sounds kind of prissy! No boy is going to say "No" to a question like "Can you handle it?")

Then you recommence. The young boy is learning a most important life skill—self-control. That he can be strong and excited but can also choose where and when to back off. For males this is very important. In adult life, a man will usually be physically stronger than his wife or female partner. He must know how to not "lose it," especially when he is angry, tired, and frustrated.

For a marriage to survive, it is sometimes necessary for partners to stand nose to nose, while saying some really honest stuff. I call this "truth time"—the time when differences that have been building up get aired and cleared away. (My wife Shaaron and I wrote a book about this, called *The Making of Love*.)

A woman can't have this kind of honest and intense discussion with a man unless she feels absolutely safe with him. She needs to know she will never be hit, and he needs to know in himself that he won't hit. (In some marriages, it's the woman who is the violent one, and the woman who needs to make this commitment.) A real man is one who is in charge of himself and his behavior. A real man can be furiously angry, and yet you feel utterly safe, standing right next to him. That's a skill that takes years to acquire. But it begins in this small way, play-wrestling on the back lawn.

Teaching Boys to Respect Women

One day, in his early to mid-teens, each boy makes a very important discovery. A lightbulb goes on above his head. It suddenly occurs to him that he is *bigger than his mother*! Even the sweetest, gentlest boy just can't help realizing, sooner or later, "*She can't make me do it!*"

STORIES FROM THE HEART

What Fathers Do

by Jack Kammer

This could be dangerous, I thought. This is Los Angeles, early June 1992. And, besides, it's getting dark.

Stranded and alone, hauling a heavy suitcase, unable to find a phone that made sense or a taxi dispatcher interested in my fare, I was running late for my plane at LAX. I decided that this was a chance I needed—no, *wanted*—to take. I approached three young Hispanic men standing outside their car in a fast-food parking lot.

But first, a little background. I had just spent four days in the mountains above Palm Springs at a conference of men who wanted to give the nation new hope for old and growing problems. We talked a lot about the importance of fathers, both as an archetypal metaphor and as a practical reality.

Back in the fast-food parking lot, I warily approached the three young, black-haired, brown-skinned men.

"How ya doing?" I said calmly and evenly. "I'm trying to get to LAX and I'm running late. The cabs and the phones aren't cooperating. How much money would you need to take me?"

They looked at each other. One of them, in a white T-shirt, said to the one who must have been the driver, "Go for it, man."

The driver hesitated.

I said, "Name a price that makes it worth your while."

He looked straight at me. "Ten bucks," he said.

"I'll give you twenty."

"Let's do it, man," said the T-shirted youth. The driver nodded and popped the trunk.

"You wanna put your suitcase here?"

"No, thanks," I answered straight back. The image of being forced empty-handed out of the car was clear in my mind. "I'd rather keep it with me."

"That's cool," the T-shirt said.

So there I was, entrusting my life to what I hoped would be "positive male energy." I was thinking we should go west to Lincoln Avenue. We headed east. Now what?

But then we turned south and soon we were on a freeway. I knew it could have been stupid, but I took out my wallet, removed a twenty, and said to the driver, "Here, I want to pay you now." The driver took it with a simple "Thanks."

"So here I am, guys," I said. "I sure hope you're going to take care of me."

T-shirt, sitting in the backseat with me, my suitcase between us, smiled knowingly, and said, "It's okay, man. We're good guys."

I nodded and shrugged. "I sure hope so, because if you're not, I'm in big trouble, aren't I?"

They all laughed, and then T-shirt spoke up. "So where you from?"

"Baltimore," I answered.

"Oh, man, it's nice back east. That's what they say. Green and everything."

I smiled and nodded, "Yeah. And back east, LA is our idea of heaven."

"Naah, it's rough here, man. It's hard." T-shirt was clearly going to be the spokesman.

Every issue we men's movement guys had talked about during our conference in the mountains was in this car. It was time for a reality check.

"How old are you guys?" I asked.

They were sixteen and seventeen. They were all in school and had part-time jobs. T-shirt and the driver worked in a restaurant. The quiet young man riding shotgun didn't say.

"Tell me about the gangs. Are there gangs at your school?"

"There's gangs everywhere, man. Everywhere. It's crazy."

"Are you guys in a gang?" I asked.

"No way, man."

"Why not?" I wondered.

"Because there's no hope in it. You just get a bullet in your head."

"Yeah, but what hope is there for you outside the gang?"

"I don't know. I just want to get a future. Do something."

"What's the difference between you guys and the guys in the gangs?"

"I don't know, man. I don't know. We're just lucky I guess."

I let the question sit for a moment, then started up. "What about fathers? Do you have a father at home?" I asked the youth in the backseat with me.

"Yeah. I do."

"How about you?" I asked the driver.

"Yeah, I got a dad."

"Living with you?"

"Yeah." And the shotgun rider volunteered, "I got a dad, too."

"How about the guys in the gangs? Do they have fathers living with them?"

"No way, man. None of them do."

"So maybe fathers make a difference?" I suggested.

"Absolutely, man. Absolutely."

"Why?" I probed. "What difference does a father make?"

"He's always behind you, man, pushing you. Keeping you in line."

"Yeah. Telling you what's what," driver and shotgun agreed.

And I was taken safely right where I needed to go. The driver even asked what terminal I wanted. On time. Without a hitch.

At the conference in the mountains I met eighteen amazing men. I am eternally grateful for their wisdom and their urge to heal the nation. But the most amazing men I met on my trip were the three youngest ones, Pablo, Juan, and Richard—amazing because, in spite of everything, they were trying to be good.

And the men to whom I am most grateful are the men I never met. The men to whom I am most grateful are their fathers. It was their fathers who got me to the airport. It was their fathers who kept me safe.

The thought leads to action and, sooner or later, the boy will try to get the best of Mom by bluffing or intimidating her, even in subtle ways. This is an important teaching moment. Don't panic; it isn't necessary to worry or get scared.

Picture this, if you will. Fourteen-year-old Sam is in the kitchen. Sam's job is to do the dishes—clear them, scrape them off, put them in the dishwasher, and switch it on. No big deal—he's done it since he was nine. But last night, he didn't finish the job. So, tonight, when his mother goes to get the dishes from the dishwasher (to serve the meal his father has cooked!) they are in there, unwashed, and looking decidedly moldy.

Sam's mom naturally calls him on it. "What happened?" But tonight Sam is fourteen! He heaves his shoulders back, he stalks about. Perhaps he speaks a little disrespectfully to his mother, under his breath.

Now let's imagine this family is really lucky. One, they have a father. Two, he's home. And three, he knows his job (we're talking miracles here)!

Sam's father is in the family room reading the paper (kind of keeping an overview of things). He picks up on what is going on in the kitchen. This is his cue! Something deep inside him has been waiting for this moment. He folds his paper, strides to the kitchen, and leans on the fridge. Sam can *feel* him come in—it's a kind of primeval moment, hormonal. He can feel the shift of power. The father looks long and hard at Sam and says some time-honored words—words that *you* probably heard when you were fourteen.

"Don't speak to your mother in that tone of voice . . ."

Now, Sam's mother is a twenty-first-century woman and is quite capable of dealing with Sam. The difference is she is not in it alone. Sam realizes that there are two adults here who respect and support each other and who are going to bring him up well. The key feeling is "gentle but firm." It's as if they are saying to Sam, *You are a good kid, but you are not raised yet. We will work on that together to help you become a fine young man.*

Most important, Sam's mother knows that she does not need to ever feel intimidated in her own home. It's *not* a physical thing between the father and son, but a kind of moral force. If the father is for real, if he respects his partner and he has credibility, then it will work every time, even if some more discussion is needed. The discussion should *not* be about the dishes, but about how to converse respectfully and safely. (If a mother is raising a boy on her own, she'll have to take a slightly different tack—this is discussed in chapter 6, "Mothers and Sons.")

Sadly, many dads don't get this aspect of their role. I've seen dads come in to this conversation and say, "Why are you picking on the kid?" or "Why are you making such an issue of it, darling?" or "Hey you guys, I can't hear the TV!" These dads are undermining their wives. This is a disaster—when a mother is doing the hard stuff and the father cuts her legs off from under her. These men are in for a terrible time. The gods, and the women, smile on those men who stand alongside them, without getting too heavy, and just add their support to the situation.

PRACTICAL HELP

Is It ADD or DDD (Dad Deficiency Disorder)?

Several years ago, a man called Don came up to me after a lecture and told me this story. Don was a truck driver and, a year earlier, his son, aged eight, had been diagnosed with Attention Deficit Disorder. Don read the diagnosis and, for want of better information, decided it meant his son Troy wasn't getting enough attention. That, surely, was what "attention deficit" meant!

Don set himself the goal of getting more involved with Troy. He had always taken the view that raising children was best left to the "missus" while he worked to pay the bills. Now all of that changed. During the holidays, and after school when possible, Troy rode in the truck with his dad. On weekends, whereas Don had often spent the time away with buddies who collected and rode classic motorcycles, Troy now came along, too.

"We had to tone down the language and clean up our act a little, but the guys all understood, and some started bringing their kids too," Don told me with a smile.

The good news: Troy calmed down so much in a couple of months that he came off his Ritalin medication—he was no longer ADD. But father and son continue to hang out together—because they enjoy it.

Note: We are not saying here that all instances of Attention Deficit Disorder are really dad-deficit disorders—but quite a lot are. (For more about ADD, ADHD, and boys, see page 198.)

Do I Have to Have
All the Answers?

When I was a young man, I studied martial arts in my spare time. I was pretty bad at it, but I liked the idea of being able to defend myself and others. Perhaps I would get a chance to rescue a beautiful maiden. The one time I got mugged, though, the mugger didn't use any of the attacks I had learned to defend against. I remember thinking—*damn, I wish he would attack me the way I was taught!* (Luckily the mugger had terrible timing, and some police actually came around the corner and arrested him.)

Being a father is rather like this. We men think we have to be completely prepared—or worse, we think if we don't know what to do, there's something wrong with us. But parenthood is all about learning from mistakes. That's how you learn. Kids keep changing, each kid is different; it's only by taking a chance and trusting your judgment that you eventually get it right. The trick is to keep wide awake and see what works, and if it doesn't, change.

As our kids reach new ages and create new challenges, we inevitably lose the reins at times. "Can they stay at their new friend's place overnight?" "Is that book suitable for them to read?" "What is a fair consequence for this misbehavior?" Sometimes it's a real tough call.

What to do? If you don't have an answer on the spot, then it's okay to stall. The best thing to do is simply talk it over with your partner or a friend. If you are both stuck, talk it over with other parents. My kids know if they hassle me I am more likely to give an unfavorable decision, so they have become more careful! But if I genuinely don't know what to do or say, I say, "Well, I'm not happy about this, but I'll sleep on it and we'll talk some more tomorrow." As long as you *always* follow up, this response works well.

Family life is a work in progress. You only get in trouble if you have to be right and you have to show them who's boss. If you are human, it goes much better.

Finding the Balance Is Hard

It's okay to be unpopular with your kids once or twice a day! If you have lots of good time together and a long history of care and involvement to draw on, then you have goodwill saved up like money in the bank. Sometimes dads are around so little, they want it all to be smooth sailing when they are there. But kids need to know when they do something wrong. It can be hard to find that middle point between hard and soft. Maybe it's about being clear, not about using power or force at all.

I have a friend who is very close to his kids, I admire and envy how natural a father he is. But he, too, gets it wrong sometimes. Paul told me once how he lost it with his twelve-year-old son after a nightmare day at work: he exploded over some small thing and sent his son off to his bedroom, yelling at him as he went. The son deserved hardly any of this, the yelling was louder than was necessary, the boy was wincing in fear; it was a disaster.

Paul stood for minutes, ashamed and red-faced at what he had done. He realized it had to be fixed. He went and sat on his son's bed. He apologized. The boy said nothing, just lay face down on the bed. But ten minutes later, the father was in the bathroom. His son walked past him on the way to brush his teeth and get ready for bed. As he passed, he said something that touched the father's heart in a most unforgettable way: "Why is it so hard to hate you?"

Off Topic: Dads and Daughters

It's not the topic of this book, but in case this is the only parenting book you ever read, here is something about girls. Mothers are the security blanket for daughters, their major support system, but dads are the self-esteem department. This is because for most girls the opposite sex is important, and you are their practice person for the opposite sex.

For this reason, you sometimes have five times the power to either bless or wound your daughter. So don't ever, whatever you do, criticize her looks, her weight, or any aspect of her appearance. Not ever. You can debate what clothes she might wear if they are too revealing, but even here, get her mother's help.

What you *can* do is spend time with her playing sports, engaging in activities, even just driving her places, and above all talk and be interested. A dad who is close to his daughter is so good for her, because he becomes the yardstick by which she measures boys. If she knows from you that she is interesting, intelligent, and worthwhile, boys have to measure up to this—which eliminates 80 percent of them right off the bat! This has to be a good investment!

Dads Do Matter

Even today, after a whole revolution in fathers' roles, people ask: Do dads matter? Can't mothers do it all?

The research supporting the importance of dads is overwhelmingly clear. Boys with absent fathers or problem fathers are statistically more likely to be violent, get hurt, get into trouble, do poorly in school, and be members of teenage gangs in adolescence. They are less likely to go on to higher education or have a good career. They marry less successfully and are less effective fathers themselves. A good mom can make up for not having a father around, but it's really, really hard work.

Fatherless daughters are more likely to have low self-esteem, have sex before they really want to, get pregnant young, be assaulted or abused, and discontinue their schooling. Families without men are usually poorer, and children of these families are likely to move downward on the socio-economic ladder. Is all this enough to convince you?

Fathering is the best thing you are ever likely to do—for your own satisfaction and joy, and for its effect on the future of other human beings. And it's good fun.

STORIES FROM THE HEART

Letter from a Father

Dear Steve,

We have had many challenges with our son, and he with us! I'm pleased to say that things are going well for him. Other parents of boys might like to share some things we have learned.

The biggest difference between Matt and his sister, Sophie, was that Matt was very impulsive and had explosive energy. When he was eight, he ran straight out in front of a car without even pausing to look. Luckily the driver had seen Matt's ball roll onto the road and was already braking hard! The car just missed him. Boys don't always think before they act.

We really got it wrong with Matt in his early teens. Because his sister had been so easy to negotiate with, we assumed he would be the same. But he just didn't do his housework, his homework, or keep to agreements about when he would be in. Reasoning wasn't enough with him—until we realized he was crying out for firm boundaries and enforced consequences. We had been threatening him, sure, but just not carrying out consequences. When we finally did this consistently (feeling pretty mean sometimes), he improved incredibly. The thing was, he was happier too. I think some boys just need this.

Something that really helped Matt was the peer support scheme. In sixth grade he had a kindergarten child to take care of and protect. This gave him a sense of importance, and he came home full of stories about his younger charge—how the little boy learned, what he got up to. We saw a whole different side to him. Then, in seventh grade, he had a high school junior as a peer support boy who watched out for him in a bullying situation, so he benefited both ways.

Around this time we learned that although he was bratty at home, the teachers thought he was great at school! So it was just that he was letting off steam with us. Lots of parents I've talked to recognize this "school angel–home devil" situation!

At around fourteen and fifteen we felt Matt was drifting into his own world—rarely talking to us, just eating and disappearing, and giving us no insight into his world of school, his friends, and so on. Our only communication seemed to be in lecturing him. Luckily we always eat dinner together at the table, and this was the one time we got to talk. We resolved to have more time together—father and son weekends away. My wife decided to get out of the negative cycle and to give compliments to Matt, not just criticisms. He responded quite warmly. I think we had been caught in a negative pattern. Boys do want to be friends; they don't want to live in their own world, which is often quite lonely.

We both benefited from a Parent Effectiveness Training course. The best things we learned were: use "I messages" (like "I was scared when you didn't come home at the agreed time. I need you to make agreements you can keep.") instead of "You are unreliable and useless! You had better come home or else!"; also how to listen to kids' problems, so they can talk them over, instead of jumping in with advice.

We are a lot happier now, and Matt is a sociable and pleasant young man instead of a surly boy. It's important never to give up with your kids. Keep learning and getting help if you are stuck. You can always improve things if you try. Kids really need you to keep communicating with them.

Geoff

In a Nutshell

1. Make the time to be a dad. In society today, men are often little more than walking wallets. You have to fight to be a real father to your kids.

2. Be active with your children—talk, play, make things, go on trips together. Seize every chance you get to interact.

3. Sometimes **A** (Attention) **D**eficit **D**isorder is actually **D** (Dad) **D**eficit **D**isorder.

4. Share the discipline with your partner. Often your son will respond more easily to you—not from fear, but from respect and wanting to please you. Don't hit or frighten boys—it just makes them mean to others.

5. A boy will copy you. He will copy your way of acting toward his mother. He will take on your attitudes (whether you are a racist, or a perpetual victim, or an optimist, or a person who cares about justice, and so on). And he will be able to show his emotions only if you can show yours.

6. Most boys love rough-and-tumble games. Use these for enjoyment and also to teach him self-control, by stopping and setting some rules whenever the game gets too rough.

7. Teach your son to respect women—and to respect himself.

CHAPTER SIX

Mothers and Sons

Remember that first quiet moment when your new baby boy was lying in your arms and you got your first real chance to look at him—gazing at his little face and body? For mothers, it sometimes takes a while to sink in that you really have a son, a boy.

Most women say they feel more confident with a baby girl. They feel they intuitively know what her needs will be. But a boy! At the birth of a son, some women will exclaim in horror, "I don't know what to *do* with a boy!" However well prepared we are rationally, the emotional response is often still, "Wow! This is unknown territory!"

The Mother's Background

Right from the start, a woman's own "male history" has an effect on her mothering. We needlessly, unconsciously set huge store on what sex a baby is. People can't even really relate to a baby until they ask what gender it is. This shouldn't matter, but it does.

Every time a mother looks at her baby boy, hears him crying for her, or changes his diaper, she is aware that he's male. So whatever maleness has meant to her will now come into the foreground.

A woman remembers her dad and how he treated her. She has the experience of brothers, cousins, and the boys she knew in school. And then all the men she has known—lovers, teachers, bosses, doctors, ministers, coworkers, and friends. All these are woven into her male history, coloring her attitude to this unsuspecting little baby boy!

Her ideas of what men are like, how men have treated her, and what she would want to be different about men all begin to affect how she acts toward her child.

As if all this weren't enough, her feelings about this baby's father also complicate the picture. As the child grows up, does he look like his father? Does that make her love him more? If she is no longer with his father, or there are problems, this can color her feelings, too. A woman may be very aware of all these feelings, or they may be totally unconscious.

How We Care for Our Baby Boy

All our earlier attitudes and beliefs about males will be reflected in our everyday care for our boy. Each time we rush to help or hold back to let him do it for himself; each time we encourage or discourage him; each time we cuddle him warmly or frown at him and walk away. All our responses

STORIES FROM THE HEART

At the Store

Julie and her son Ben, age eight, were in town to do some supermarket shopping. Just outside the shop they saw two girls from Ben's class at school, sitting on the bench. Ben gave a cheery "Hi" to the girls, but instead of saying "Hi" back, both girls just looked at the ground and giggled!

Julie and Ben finished their shopping and went on down the street. Julie noticed that Ben was rather quiet and asked how he was doing. "Oh, I'm fine," said Ben (who, after all, is an all-American male and obligated to say this!).

Julie wasn't convinced. "Did it upset you that those girls just laughed and didn't say hello?"

"Umm . . . yes," admitted Ben.

Julie thought for a moment before replying. "Hmm—well, I don't know if this helps, but I remember being a girl in the third grade. We each did have our favorite boy. But it was kind of awkward. If he spoke to you, especially if you had friends around, you might get embarrassed. So you just might giggle to cover it up. I don't know if that fits here or not."

Ben didn't say anything, but he seemed to be walking taller all of a sudden!

"Anyhow, it's lucky," Julie went on, "that we've forgotten the milk! So we have to go back!" And before Ben could even gasp, she turned right there on the sidewalk and headed back to the supermarket. "You'll get a second chance!" she explained.

The girls were still there; this time they gave their own cheery "Hi," and Ben had a conversation with them while his mother searched for the milk—which took a while to find!

arise from our internal attitudes toward having a baby—and having a *male* baby.

It's a big help if you adopt an attitude of curiosity—of wanting to learn and understand about a boy's world. As a woman, you cannot know what it's like to be in a male body. If you didn't have brothers (or a dad who was involved), then you have to get more information to find out what is normal in boys. It's good to be able to ask your husband or male friends for information. Sometimes you just need practical knowledge.

Moms Help with Learning about the Opposite Sex

As the supermarket story (see page 101) shows, a mother teaches a boy a great deal about life and love. She is invaluable for helping him gain confidence with the opposite sex. She is his "first love"; she needs to be tender, respectful, and playful, without wanting to own or dominate his world. As he gets to school age, she encourages and helps him make friends and gives him clues about how to get along well with girls.

Many boys and girls have trouble getting along with the opposite sex, as do men and women. So a mother can help make sure her son is not like this. She can help him relax around girls and women. She can teach him what girls like— they love a boy who can converse, who has a sense of humor, who is considerate, who has his own ideas and opinions but is interested in theirs, and so on. She can even alert him to the fact that girls can sometimes be mean or thoughtless—that girls are no saints either.

The opposite-sex parent often holds the key to self-esteem for a growing child. Teenage daughters need their father to boost their image of themselves as intelligent and interesting people. He can also teach them to change a wheel, fix a computer, or catch fish (whichever of these things he knows how to do!). A son whose mother enjoys him as a companion learns that he can be friends with girls comfortably in the years from five to fifteen. The pressure to pair up and prove oneself sexually is taken away, and he can move more naturally through friendship to a deeper connection with a girl when he is ready.

The Gift of a Good Self-Image

Many boys become painfully awkward by the time they are in high school. They seem ashamed of being male, of being big and full of hormones. The media continually portrays males as rapists, murderers, or inadequate fools. So a boy may easily feel quite bad about himself as a masculine being.

Mothers can do a lot to overcome this. I've heard beautiful comments from mothers to their sons: telling them from the age of about ten and upward, "Wow, you are a great-looking guy!" when they try on their new clothes; or "The girl who marries you is going to be so lucky," when they do a good job around the house; and "I really enjoy your company," "You're interesting to talk to," and "You have a really great sense of humor." From these comments, the boy learns what girls like, and becomes more able to approach them in a relaxed and equal way.

STORIES FROM THE HEART

Letter from a Mother

Dear Steve,

Reading the manuscript of *Raising Boys*, I wanted to add some things I feel so strongly about.

To all the mothers out there—boys are different. So persevere in getting to understand and know them. Don't, whatever you do, give up. Or become resigned and join the anti-boy group with their weak jokes and tales of woe, and "What can I do?" sort of attitudes. There is a meeting point between mothers and sons. It's up to you. It may not be obvious, it may take time and a number of attempts. Struggle is not a sign of failure, but of something new being born. Look for the good in your son. You will find it.

Boys have tender feelings, and mothers have an essential part in keeping the child whole. Seeing how affectionate they can be at times makes you love them so much more. Give them a chance to play with and help younger children, and to look after animals. See how loving they can be.

Share your son's passions. Tom (my nine-year-old) and I have a wintertime ritual. On a Saturday afternoon we go to the second half of the local football game (which is about the right amount of time for us) and get in for free. We generally sit down by the fence near our team's goal line, close enough to feel the earth and air move as they surge past. Tom takes great pleasure in telling me who the players are and the rules, and I notice he often tells me the details he knows will interest me. Something about their lives outside football! The action is great, so vigorous and determined. The atmosphere at the historic ground is friendly and excited, a bubble of warmth on a cold afternoon. So different from watching it on TV! It's an urban adventure.

Boys often need help in connecting with things—with a piece of work at school, with using the library, computers, newspapers, encyclopedias. Help them to organize their homework, partition the task into doable chunks, set realistic goals, and help them to get there. Make the task smaller so they can relate to it, so they don't feel overwhelmed and give up. At the same time, don't take over—make sure they have the joy of their own achievement.

Expand your boys' awareness. Walking, talking, noticing things, collecting things. Seeing how a tree changes with the seasons, how a building project is developing. Show them how food happens—planning the purchases, choosing the fruit, the preparation and enjoyment of new foods. Involve them in planning family events and holidays. Show them how to combine their interests with those of others in a plan.

Make sure they get enough sleep and a balance of social and quiet time. Basic but critical. Bedtime rituals, stories, cuddles, tickling on the back, whatever, to feel safe, loved, and at peace. A shared repertoire of favorite stories is invaluable.

Finally, you can really help your sons by supporting their relationship with their father. Fathers may not foresee and plan the way you do, and this may limit their opportunities to what is nearest at hand. Gentle reminders can be appreciated. Put good men in the path of your son—a groovy music teacher, a valued handyman, a friend's brother. Speak to them about good men, their qualities, and what you notice about how they act in different situations.

Recall their past—tell them what a beautiful baby they were, what their birth meant to you, what a ray of sunshine they are in your life, a deep harmony, a beautiful boy.

With warm wishes,
Judi

Adjusting Your Mothering to Their Growing Up

As a boy grows from helpless baby to towering teenager, your parenting style has to adjust with him. To begin with, you're "the boss," providing constant supervision. In the school years you teach, monitor, and set limits. Later you are a consultant and friend as he makes his own way. You gradually grant him more and more responsibility and freedom. It's all in the timing. Here are some clues to the process.

THE ELEMENTARY SCHOOL YEARS

In the primary school years a lot of gentle steering and helping goes on. Mothers watch their sons' activities for dangers or for the risk of an imbalance. They set a limit to their TV viewing or computer time, so they get out and exercise. (Many schools have banned computer play during lunch breaks because some boys never learn to socialize or interact—skills that they really need.)

Encourage your son to invite friends over, and be kind to and chat with them. Feeding them always helps! Ask them for their points of view and their ideas about school and their lives.

It's okay and important to monitor and check who will be there when they visit a friend's house. Are they well supervised? Boys can get into deep water if no one looks out for them at this age. They shouldn't be left alone in a house for long, under the age of ten. (This depends a lot on where you live.) Riding bikes around after dark is not good. And boys under ten are not yet ready for the traffic on main roads. Their peripheral (side) vision is not fully developed for judging traffic speeds.

PRACTICAL HELP

Little Boys' Bodies

Penises and testicles are a bit of a mystery for mothers. Here are a doctor's answers to some questions mothers commonly ask:

Q: Should my son have two testicles visible?

A: By the six-week check-up that all babies should get, both testicles should be visible.

Q: Is it okay to touch his penis to wash it?

A: Of course! You have to wash around the penis and testicles when changing diapers and in the bath. Once out of diapers, a little boy can wash his own penis while you supervise.

Q: Should I pull back the foreskin to keep his penis really clean?

A: This is not necessary; in fact, it's not a good idea at all. At this age the foreskin is adhered to the end of the penis. Toddlers naturally pull back the foreskin little by little, and at about three or four years of age you will notice that it retracts. At the age of four, you can tell him from time to time in the bath to pull it back and wash around the end of his penis. Show him how to leave the foreskin back until he is dry after a shower, and how to pull the foreskin back when urinating to keep urine from collecting underneath it.

Q: My son pulls and stretches his penis or pushes his finger inside it. Is this okay?

A: Basically, children won't damage themselves, because if it hurts they'll soon stop! Penises are a little fascinating to their owners and feel comforting to hold. All this is fine—don't make a fuss about it.

PRACTICAL HELP *(CONTINUED)*

Q: My son often holds onto his penis to stop himself from peeing. Is that harmful?

A: Most boys do this. Girls have strong pelvic muscles that can hold back their pee without anyone knowing they're doing it. Boys are made differently, so they can't do this. So if they need to pee but are too engrossed in playing, they will often "hang on" with hands. Encourage him to take a toilet break!

Q: What name should we call our child's penis?

A: Call a penis a penis. Don't make up silly names for it.

Q: When boys are a little older, they sometimes get hit in the testicles during games. What should I do?

A: Testicles are very sensitive—that's why all the men crouch over in sympathy if one of them gets hit in the crotch. But usually there is no lasting damage. Go with your boy to a private spot and check him out gently. If there is severe pain, swelling, bleeding, or bruising, or if pain continues to make him cry for a long time, or if he vomits, get him straight to a doctor. Otherwise, just let him sit quietly and recover. If there is still tenderness after a few hours, have him checked by a doctor.

If you are in any doubt about these questions, talk to your doctor. It's always best to be on the safe side.

Always encourage children to be careful of each other's bodies. Challenge your son or daughter strongly if they think harming other kids is funny or trivial. Come down hard on games that involve grabbing or hitting people in the genitals. Some TV shows recently have treated these injuries almost as a joke, which they are not—it's just part of the anti-male trend in the media these days. Being hit in the genitals is about as funny as being hit in the breasts, and testicles are far more sensitive.

(Our thanks to Dr. Nick Cooling for this information.)

Junior High and High School

By secondary school, living with a boy is more a matter of fair exchange—"I'll drive you there if you help me out here," "If you cook, I'll clean up." A boy can have much more separation of his activities and yours. But stay friendly and available so talking can still happen. Be sure to still have special times one-on-one. Stop for a snack and talk on shopping trips. Go out to movies together and take time afterward to talk.

Some boys still love cuddling at this age; others find it too intrusive. Find ways to show affection that are respectful of his wishes. Sit close on the couch, stroke his head at bedtime, tickle him—find the ways that he doesn't mind.

You may have to make a stand against a school activity or sport dominating your kid's life too much (see "Homework Hell," page 158). Allow your son to have a "health day" or two once a term—a day off from school when he doesn't have to be sick but can be peaceful by himself.

Toward the end of high school, during the pressure of major exams, help your son study but take a position that this alone is not the meaning of life and that enjoyment and soul time are also important. Let him know his worth is not measured by exam results.

A kind of competitive madness has developed around test results, SAT scores, and the like. It's portrayed as the make-or-break event of a person's life. We can take a middle road here, encouraging kids to give school their best shot but keeping it in proportion with the real goals of adolescence—which are to find what work you really love to do, while also developing socially and creatively.

Here are some points to consider:

- Kids who get high test scores in their senior year often struggle in college because they aren't motivated by actual interest in the subjects.
- For advanced courses like medicine, schools are starting to look for more balanced students who have done other degrees first or had other life experiences. Students with good exam results don't necessarily make good doctors.
- Well-balanced youngsters become happier, healthier, and more likable employees and become more successful in professional careers.
- Other courses and careers (such as teaching, nursing, and ecology) often offer happier lifestyles and more human satisfaction than the highly competitive fields like law, medicine, and economics.

Learning Through Consequences

This is the age of building personal responsibility—which has to be learned through consequences. For instance, when your son starts high school, help him get organized with books and catching the bus. But once he knows how, after a while, it's up to him if he takes the wrong book or misses the bus and is late. He'll soon learn!

Discipline works by cooperation. Natural consequences and a sense of fairness are your tools. Negotiate with him. You can't *make* a teenager do things by force—but you provide so many services that your bargaining power is huge!

PRACTICAL HELP

Boys in the Kitchen

It's easy to start kids off with a lifetime interest in food preparation, because nature is on your side. Kids love to eat. They love the smells, colors, tastes, and even the mess of food!

Babies can sit on the floor in the kitchen rolling oranges around or piling pea pods in and out of a plastic bowl. Toddlers can help you make play dough (not to eat!), stirring and kneading the mixture, adding bright coloring. Then they can have hours of fun playing with the results.

For four- or five-year-olds, Christmas and party treats are the most motivating cooking (because you get to eat them!). Making cookies and icing a cake are both good kids' activities. Never let them near a stove or hot things on their own, though.

Little boys can stir, pour, measure, or weigh, shuck sweet corn, shell peas, and wash carrots and potatoes in a plastic washbowl. (Growing vegetables in the garden is another great possibility. Radishes grow the fastest. Snow peas, cherry tomatoes, and strawberries are good because you can pick more every day.) Boys love to make faces on bread with strips of carrot and celery, sliced tomato, and cheese shapes. They also love freezing juice to make their own ice pops. When a little older, they can safely use a peeler on veggies to help out at mealtime.

Kids need to be around ten years old before they can use sharp knives, hot liquids, or stoves. You should teach them, watch how they do, then check that they are still being careful. It's best to have just one child at a time in the kitchen when cooking with hot things.

Meals Boys Like to Cook

- Pizzas—buy the dough and let them add a variety of toppings
- Grilled fish sticks, chicken, sausages, chops, or tofu

- Pancakes and omelets

- Tossed salads

- Hamburgers or steak sandwiches with salad

- Pasta and bottled sauce

- Roast lamb or chicken

- Stir-fried vegetables and rice

- Tuna patties made with instant mashed potato, canned tuna, and grated carrot or celery

Be sure to show lots of pride in their work and your appreciation of their help in the kitchen. Show them how they can make a gift (such as a cake or a batch of cookies) for someone they like.

Don't forget they also need to see men as well as women working in the kitchen.

Other Safety Tips

Teach your boys to:

- Wash their hands before they start!

- Handle knives with lots of care.

- Clean up spilled food immediately, particularly on the floor (so they won't slip in it!).

- Be alert to what gets hot and stays hot during cooking (use an oven mitt for picking up hot things).

- Turn saucepan handles to the side of the stove where they won't be bumped or grabbed by a toddler.

- Roll up their sleeves and wear an apron (or clothes that won't brush against a burner and catch fire).

(See Notes section for our recommended cookbooks for kids.)

Single Mothering: Avoiding Conflicts That Can Do Harm

For a mother on her own, the mid-teens are an important time to renegotiate what is happening. Boys at this age are wanting to test their strength and gain some independence. For a couple, this is easier—a boy can fight with his dad but know his mother still loves him (and vice versa). But if Mom is the only source of love *and* discipline, it takes real care.

Many mothers have told us, "I have to keep switching back and forth—being hard and soft, hard and soft. It's really tiring." (However, this is better than having a partner who contradicts you and undermines your discipline.) *It's important never to let things get as far as a yelling or hitting match with your son.* At this age, when he is learning to handle his own energies and feelings, he might hurt you and feel terrible afterward. If you can see a discussion turning into a shouting match or a physical fight, then do the following:

1. Tell him *we both* need to calm down. Make some coffee or a cool drink, sit down, and talk it over rationally.

2. If you are feeling too angry or upset, tell him that you will come back to the subject later—when you feel less emotional.

3. Go and sit down, or have something to drink, or go to another room.

4. Try to act before you are actually upset—if you wait until you are crying or very angry, he will feel guilty and confused.

5. Later in the day, have a talk with him. Set aside the original problem to begin with. Talk about the bigger issue of being able to get along well in the household and how important that is. Ask if he, too, wants to get along well. Explain that this sometimes involves compromises. The things you *won't* compromise on are those concerning safety, his keeping agreements he makes, and respecting the rights of others in the family. Ask if he is willing to always stop and calm down if you ask him to do so. Then you can either have a break to celebrate or talk about the original problem.

By doing something like this, you are saying, in effect, "For a mother and a teenage son, it's necessary to make some truces, because the situation is delicate."

If your son is hitting you or intimidating you, then get help from a counselor or, if necessary, the police. A single mother is the main source of love for her child, boy or girl, and if they hurt or harm you, you will both feel very bad. Yet growing up requires testing limits with someone. Ideally, uncles or adult friends of yours whom the boy trusts may talk to him about treating you with respect. If they can do this without laying a big guilt trip on him, that's great. Ideally, uncles or grandfathers will be spending time with him, so that they may already have his trust and respect.

Sharing a Boy with His Dad

Many mothers make the discovery that they can either help or hinder their boys' relationship with his father. This wonderful letter (see page 116) tells how a mother realized she was

STORIES FROM THE HEART

Making Room for a Dad to Grow

Dear Steve,

I'm writing this because I thought you would enjoy hearing about the impact of your book, *Manhood*, on our family. It can all be summed up in one particular scene, which still sits so clearly in my mind.

My husband, Joe, and I were sitting at a table outside a restaurant at our usual holiday location. We love to get to the beach for a couple of weeks and take our four boys ages nine to eighteen along with us.

As we were sitting drinking our coffee, I looked over the road and suddenly saw both of our older teenage boys sneaking into the liquor store! When I leaped up to deal with them my husband rose, too, and with an unfamiliar firmness said, "I'll deal with this." I was so stunned the best I could offer was a feeble protest. I sat back down and watched him go!

I should explain here that for many years, Joe has been the "quiet achiever," supporting the family. But in the interpersonal department—handling the boys—I was always the one who did the parenting. Sometimes I found this easy, but sometimes very hard.

I knew that Joe had just finished reading your book *Manhood*, which I'd brought along on the holiday to read. I wondered if this had something to do with his sudden change of behavior. When he returned from sorting out the boys, I asked him how he had found the book. (Hoping of course he'd learned all the lessons I intended him to!) His words still ring in my ears. *"Well, mostly I realize I've allowed you to come between the boys and me, and I no longer plan to allow that to happen!"*

My second reaction (my first was "That's not what you were supposed to learn!") was to defend my actions! But almost as soon as I started, I knew he was right. In my efforts to raise these boys to be the sort of men I thought they should be, I had endeavored to protect them from what I thought would harm them. Sadly, I think eighteen years ago I was right, but what I had failed to acknowledge and trust was that *their dad had grown to be the type of man I wanted them to be and I hadn't noticed.* What a sobering moment.

As I've integrated this learning, I've shared it with other women too. I now believe it's the gap many strong women fall into. *We convince ourselves we are a vital bridge between our husbands and sons, when in fact we have become a barrier.*

This has given me the confidence to stand back and allow their relationships to develop, and develop they have. Our younger boys have especially benefited. I now allow Joe to intervene when we hit the "you can't make me do it" wall and continue to be astounded at how effective his intervention is. Not only has this allowed Joe's relationship with the boys to grow, but also a much more mutual respect between us as to what we both offer as parents.

It hasn't been easy for me to stand back, and under pressure I often still revert to old behavior. The difference is Joe's confidence has grown with practice and he stands up to me! He is an equal parent now, and I love it!

Lynn

PRACTICAL HELP

Introducing a New Partner

Divorce can be tough on a boy, and if his mother finds a new partner it can also be a big adjustment. In his book, *The Wonder of Boys*, Michael Gurian offers some strategies for mothers who are remarrying after divorce. The following summary of his guidelines is a good starting point for consideration.

1. **Taking care about dating behavior.** A mother shouldn't expose her son to myriad male influences. She should bring a new man into the boy's life only when she's ready to invest in a long-term attachment.

2. **Not displacing Dad.** The new man should not be seen as a substitute for Dad. Discipline structures and household routines that are imposed by the stepfather have to be explained clearly to the son and imposed as additions to, not substitutes for, his father's and mother's rules and routines.

3. **Mending fences with Dad.** A mother should confront her part in the marriage breakup, mend fences with the father, and include him in plans and arrangements. Both she and the father should rise above any difficult situations between them for the good of the boy.

4. **Supporting living with Dad.** The mother may, when the son asks for it, let him go and live with his dad. As the boy moves into his teens, she may need to offer this so that the son will feel okay about asking.

5. **Making it clear that your new man is not a competitor.** A mother needs to reassure her son that he is irreplaceable in her life. She does this with her time, words, and actions, not by buying his approval with gifts or treats.

The golden rules are: keep communicating, keep your family rituals strong, and spend time together as parent and child. The greatest gift that parents can give a son in this situation is their own stability.

"getting in the way," and how much easier life was when she allowed her husband to share the parenting burdens—and rewards.

Equality of the Sexes

Most women are determined to raise their sons and daughters equally. Today's mothers are from a generation that was awakened to male chauvinism and equal rights. We absolutely bristle if we see our sons acting rudely to a girl and are positively incensed if our son is arrogant or cruel. But we also feel the other side of the coin—a stab of pain if our son is ignored in the school yard, or if he comes home distressed about the humiliation received from the girls in his class or (a few years down the road) the woman in his life.

So we walk this fine line. Affirming him as a person, yet not allowing him to be too full of himself.

In a Nutshell

1. Giving birth to a boy brings to the surface how you feel about males in general. Be careful not to land too many prejudices on this innocent little boy.

2. If you aren't experienced with males (for example, if you didn't grow up with brothers), then ask men to tell you what it's like being male. Don't be afraid of little boys' bodies!

3. Little boys learn love from their mothers. Be kind and warm, and enjoy them.

4. Teach your boy about girls and how to get along well with them.

5. Praise your son's looks and conversation so he feels good about himself.

6. Adjust your parenting as your son gets older. Keep a close eye on safety and the healthy balance of his life, stepping back more as he gets into his teens, but never losing contact with his world, his concerns, and whether he is getting out of his depth.

7. In adolescence, let him learn from the consequences of his actions (or inactions), such as being late for school if he dawdles. This is the age for learning more about responsibility.

8. Encourage an affinity with food preparation from an early age, then enjoy the results. Being of service is the key to lifelong self-esteem.

9. Take care not to have big fights in adolescence, especially if you are a single mother. Calm down, then return to the issue logically.

10. If you are a strong, capable kind of mom, then be careful that you don't displace your husband from being close to the kids or doing his part of the parenting. You and your boys need him involved. Encourage your sons and their father to grow close.

PRACTICAL HELP

Getting Boys to Do Housework

There are several reasons why housework is very good for boys.

Preparing Them for Independent Living

It's not healthy for a boy to go straight from living with his parents to living with a partner. An interval of independent living is strongly advised. During this time, he will sometimes need to iron and vacuum and prepare something to eat! These skills should be learned during the formative younger years, lest serious learning disabilities like "kitchen blindness" or "dyslaundria" begin to develop.

In a boy's late teens, these skills will play a critical role in other ways, too. Housework skills are up there with a sports car in the "chick-magnet" stakes. As a general rule, cook and clean and tidy for your late-teenage son only if you want him to *stay at home for the rest of your life!*

Even marriage may not solve your son's domestic needs. The woman (or man) he eventually links up with in this post-modern world may reject the idea of becoming a household servant to your son. There's a distinct and frightening possibility that he will have to do his share on a lifelong basis.

Real Self-Esteem

From the moment you first see a TV screen or billboard, your mental health is under attack.

On average, we each see about three thousand advertising messages a day, and they all tell us we are not good enough, that we should be dissatisfied with our looks and our lives. Advertising attacks your children's mental health. It tells them that self-esteem is about how you look and what you own.

The sports stars and fashion models our kids admire actually have terrible self-esteem; they know that it can all disappear overnight. So how do we make our kids feel good about them-selves? The secret is easy: teach them to be useful.

It's important to tell kids they are great, smart, and able to think and figure things out. But that's only the first step. Being able to cook a meal, iron a shirt, look after a pet, mow enough lawns to buy a computer, and hold down a part-time job are all sources of indestructible pride. We should give our kids lots of chances to experience their capabilities.

As a guideline, we suggest teaching your son to prepare a complete evening meal every week by the time he is ten. Per-haps start with pasta and prepared sauce, with a simple dessert. (Don't allow boys to handle boiling water earlier than about nine years of age, as they aren't coordinated enough to do it safely. Nine is the age at which a boy's attention span overtakes that of a border collie! Under nine, it's best to have them peel, wash, clean, and do other things to help.) Little boys from about five onward should start setting the silverware for meals and finding and folding their clothes from the laundry pile. Seven-year-olds can clear the table, and so on.

When a teenage boy experiences the pride of being useful to his family, his relatives, and to the wider community of people who like and respect him, he never loses that feeling. It will affect which friends he chooses, his choice of subjects at school, his girlfriend or wife, his career. So you can see just how important that first batch of pasta and jarred sauce is going to be!

A Chance to Get Close

There's another reason to teach your boys housework on a regu-lar basis, which may surprise you. It's conversation.

Boys don't often leap into a frank and honest discussion of their educational progress, friendship traumas, or love life the minute they walk in the door. This has long been a source of frustration to mothers and fathers eager to catch up with their son's life. This is because males like to talk "sideways" rather than face-to-face. They like to be engaged in some useful activity, which takes their attention, while talking to someone working alongside them. This gives them time to search for the right words, and none of that embarrassing eyeball-to-eyeball stuff that women like to engage in.

If you want to get close to your son and help him to off-load his worries or share his joys, you have to do things together. In modern life, that usually means housework. Whether you are helping your son whip up a delicious soufflé for dinner or teaching him how to get a really good shine on the shower stall later that night, these are the times that he will begin to tell you about his problems with math or the girl who is chasing him. (We know of one family that refuses to buy a dishwasher because they love the conversation at the sink. We think this is madness, but admirable all the same!)

Quite seriously, doing work with your son—teaching him the tricks of doing it well, how to be fast and efficient and happy in making life cleaner and tidier—is a way that a parent and child can enjoy each other, have good long talks, and pass on all kinds of wisdom. If you do all the housework for your son, then you miss out, and so does he.

CHAPTER SEVEN

Developing a Healthy Sexuality

We all want our boys to feel good about their sexuality and able to enjoy it in an intimate, loving, and joyful way. But we also want them to be wide awake about the hazards that accompany sex if it isn't approached with care. Added to the perennial risks of unwanted pregnancy and STDs is the additional problem of HIV/AIDS. These are very good reasons to want our sons to keep their brains on when they take off their clothes!

Love is powerful and often very confusing, too. The simplest and most helpful thing young people need to understand is that there are three kinds of attraction:

liking is a mental spark, shared beliefs and preferences, and the connection with another mind

loving is tender, warm, melting, a heartfelt emotion

lusting is spicy, hot, hungry, aching, tingling—need we go on?

Young love has a lot to do with sorting out which is which. Mistakes are inevitable; the trick is to go slowly enough to be able to sort out which is which. Parents can help by keeping the brakes on just enough to allow a young person some thinking space. If teenagers are insecure or can't talk to adults about their choices, they may easily rush ahead of their own inner feelings. The overwhelming sexualization of our world by the corporate media through television, music videos, billboards, and magazines often makes young people feel pressured to be sexual when they don't really feel ready. Lasting relationships are the ones that take time to grow.

Teenagers (and other slow learners!) fall in love quickly. In adolescence, we are often so hungry to be in love that we color anyone who seems a likely candidate in the bright hues of our imagination. We are "in love with love" as much as with the actual person. In time, the real person shows through and the fantasy meets the reality. Which could be good—as real people are much more interesting. Or it could be bad—but at least you've found out!

When it comes to sex, one ethic says it all: never intentionally harm or misuse somebody else. Young people need lots of warmth, positive support, and good practical information—and a chance to grow up before becoming sexually active.

The Essential Goodness of Sex

We want our boys to feel good about being male and about being sexual. But very negative messages come flooding in from the media, especially the news media. A teenager may see TV news about rape in Darfur or pedophiles in the Church. He may read about horrific sex crimes in the paper. For pre-adolescent boys, the feelings must be very unsettling. By thirteen or fourteen most boys have strong sexual feelings and a fascination with the images of women that are presented all around them. The testosterone now surging in their bodies makes a boy's pelvic area tingle and stir. Boys at this age generally masturbate at least once a day. The sexual energy they carry is enormous. Yet nothing positive is being done to honor this new part of their life. It's often not even discussed. As a result, boys are full of doubts. They wonder if a girl will ever be interested in them, if their intentions are honorable, or if they are just another rapist waiting to explode!

Sexual learning includes two parts: the physical details of lovemaking and the much bigger questions of attitudes and values. The practical aspects of sex should be covered in conversations and explanations with your children from toddlerhood onward. The really potent information about sex is the *attitude* you bring to it. This has to come from parents and the adult community. If you don't talk about sex (and right and wrong), teenagers will take their values from friends and TV. Be clear with your boys that there is good sex (respectful, happy, close, careful about pregnancy and STDs) and bad sex (using others selfishly).

How People Get Hurt When Sex Isn't Honored

In my high school class (like in every high school class since the beginning of time) there was a girl whose breasts grew larger and earlier than the other girls' did. Two boys in our class who were a little older than the others and sat at the back of the class would catcall crudely every time Jeannie walked into the classroom. It became a real obsession with them, and I think we all wished they would stop. Jeannie was quite outgoing up until this time, but you could see her confidence trickle away—they made her life miserable. I wished we had had a strong enough boy culture to tackle them, to tell them to stop, to confront the stupidity and cruelty of it.

In another instance, a good friend of mine at school, Joseph, was Maltese. Because he was a little short, or just because he was an immigrant, some of the class took to calling him gay, and made a game of ducking away from him in the playground, guarding their backsides. Joe became more and more of an outsider, and eventually quit school.

When I look back on these times, I feel regret and shame at not speaking up. Talk to your kids about this, and when they use derogatory words or insults, confront them about it. These terms are too harmful to be given the excuse of just joking. A lot of boys' "creep" behavior stems more from ignorance or thoughtlessness—it isn't really sinister. Adults or wiser boys need to simply say something casual but clear-cut—and stop the abuse. Younger boys are wired to take their cues from older ones, or from men, and the practice will stop. Boy culture is just the blind leading the blind so much of the time,

PRACTICAL HELP

Rite of Passage

A Ceremony for Honoring the Beginning of Adolescence and Giving Sexuality a Positive Start

Authors Don and Jeanne Elium describe a ritual that we thought was a great idea and adapted it for use in our own family. The Eliums were unhappy that boys often get sexual messages first from the school yard and that these messages might color a boy's attitude. They felt they needed to be proactive.

What the Eliums suggest is to set aside a day to celebrate entering adolescence; about ten years of age is a good time. (This may seem a little young, but in our society this is when adolescent pressures begin. It's the time when sexually explicit conversations occur between children at school and often misinformed attitudes begin to develop.) Tell your son in advance that you are planning a celebration evening with him. The highlight will be a special meal at a restaurant that he chooses—a real grown-up restaurant, not fast food.

When the day comes, before heading to the restaurant, arrange some time for both parents to sit and talk together with him. It's a good idea to plan ahead and clarify with each other what you are going to say. (This is not a good time to have an argument!) If you are a single parent, this will still work just fine—in fact, it may be easier.

When you are all sitting down together, talk to your son about sex and what it means to you.

Not "the birds and the bees" (which he should already know about), but the experience of it—where it fits into your own life. Be as personal as you can. (We certainly found this quite challenging. Our son was a little embarrassed and longing for it to be over, though this is true of any initiatory experience and doesn't mean it's a bad idea.)

Each partner can speak about how he or she feels about sex. They can pass on the message that sex is great and that their son will enjoy it—from masturbation to begin with, to later on (*much later on*, mothers tend to emphasize!) when he enters a relationship with a partner. (It's worth mentioning here that at this age you don't know if your child is going to be heterosexual, so some easygoing, nonjudgmental acknowledgment of other possibilities would be great to cover all bases!)

You (parents, that is) may want to drink some Champagne while you are sitting together. Then it's on to celebrate becoming an adolescent. The parents and this child only (no other children) go out for the meal. Your son might like to invite some special adults in his life—friends or relatives—who he would really like to come along, too. Have some talk during the second half of the meal about how great it is that he is growing up (but not with a sexual emphasis), and spend some time reminiscing about his younger life and the funny and memorable parts of it. You and the other adults might bring photos. Whatever you do, it's meant to be a fun night. One that gives your son a sense of being special and taking on new responsibilities. A kind of honoring of him as no longer being a child. (Some cultures do this at the time of a girl's first period, and girls tell us that although they feel embarrassed, they also find it really special.)

YOU DID WHAT ?

and behavior usually sinks to the lowest denominator. Robert Bly calls it a "sibling society" with no elders.

Peer pressure can work for good as well as bad. Several times in my youth I saw young men speak up and prevent rapes from taking place. Vietnam vets have told me about how, during the course of that war, they talked comrades out of committing atrocities when overcome with grief or anger. One example: Fellow soldiers landing in helicopters confronted the infamous My Lai massacre murderers and saved hundreds of innocents from being killed. Keeping each other out of trouble is a big part of how men help each other.

It takes skill to steer things in a better direction in a group situation. Kids can learn these skills only if they have seen someone else handling a similar situation well. When I worked in schools, I noticed that if a child was hurt accidentally while playing a sport, often one of the bigger boys would

be very caring and helpful. At other times, though, when no boy with these qualities was present, the group would just laugh and add humiliation to injury, or be awkward and look away if a smaller boy was really distressed. The boys who helped often came from large families where they had kid sisters and brothers and, I guess, were used to taking a nurturing role. They were more well-rounded human beings and good to have around.

Someone to Talk To

A big problem for many boys is the difficulty they have in talking about personal matters with their friends. They miss all the support, clarification, and relief that comes from conversations of a deeper kind. In my boyhood, no discussion ever seemed to go deeper than last night's episode of *Mission Impossible*. Girls, on the other hand, talked things through endlessly. There were many problems we boys could have talked over. The boy I sat next to in class was often beaten up by his alcoholic father. Another's parents divorced messily during his senior year. I only learned of these things many years later, yet I spent thousands of hours with these boys.

If parents—especially dads, uncles, and grandfathers, as well as mothers—talk to their boys openly and listen to their problems, there is a better chance that the boys will carry these skills into their peer group. What a difference that would make!

How Boys Feel about Girls

Boys in their mid-teens think that girls are wonderful. They envy the easy way girls laugh and talk with their friends, their savvy and their physical grace. But above all, they are aware of girls' tantalizing sexual promise. Added to this heady brew is a strong romantic streak that many boys have. They can invest a real spiritual intensity into idealizing a particular girl as the epitome of everything noble and pure.

But something gets in the way of everyday relating to real girls. Girls make conversation more easily than boys do. It's hard for boys to know what to say to them. And in high school, the girls are much more mature physically than the boys of the same age. They appear like goddesses to the boys who are mostly little nerds with hollow chests and short legs!

Girls seem to hold all the cards. Many boys (especially the nonathletic, the ill-clad, those with big noses or fat or skinny legs) begin to think they aren't ever going to make it with a girl. They feel destined to be losers in the romantic stakes. This sits very heavily on their minds.

Of course, unknown to the boys, the girls too are often feeling uncertain and awkward. They would actually like to talk, mix, and share affection with the boys. If the boys were a little more socially skilled or bolder, many more affirming things could happen between the genders. Instead, the girls whisper to each other and mock the boys, the boys harass and trash the girls, and the quiet ones stand back from it all and brood.

For most kids, this is just depressing and sad. Eventually, some confidence develops and things improve. But for some young men a "creep" mentality sets in. ("If I can't meet girls as equals, I'll have to control them.") This isn't helped by the phenomena of degradingly graphic Internet and magazine porn, or even music videos that use girls as "eye candy" to sell songs. Showing someone something they can't have is cruel and abusive. This, deep down, feeds a strong, sexually charged and understandable anger. If boys don't get much chance to talk and engage with real girls, and experience respect and liking from them, they are more likely to start to fantasize about control and domination. Their attitude toward women, and their ability to relate to girls as people, just gets worse.

The men's movement shares with the women's movement an anger at the use of images in advertising that grab our sons by the penis, so to speak. Sometimes this pushes them over the edge. Some years ago, in Australia where I live, a world-famous supermodel launched a line of lingerie at a big department store, complete with raunchy music and gyrating models. A young man jumped onto the stage during the fashion parade and called out, "You whore!" before security guards evicted him. He then went and threw himself to his death from a tall building.

A young man's heart is not unconnected from his pelvis but, as one young man wrote, "the pictures never love you back." The end point of this "creepification" process is the young man who rapes a girl, or the adult who sexually assaults children.

Parents are angered by the manipulation of their kids. Parents of younger children are turning off the TV sets or not buying even ordinary magazines.

A great many men carry from boyhood a huge inferiority complex in the area of sex and romance. It makes them poor lovers, and their wives may soon lose interest. This makes the men desperate for sex; being desperate makes them unlovable; and being unlovable makes them desperate all over again. This may well be the cause of most marriage breakups. Boyhood is the time when some positive words, some affection, and some honor from parents and friends can make all the difference to a boy's long-term happiness.

How Boys Shut Down Their Bodies

Have you noticed the way boys begin shutting down their feelings once they reach school age? Little boys are full of feelings and energies. But in the jungle of the school yard they soon grow ashamed of useful and healthy emotions like sadness, fear, and tenderness. To make himself cope, a boy suppresses his feelings and tenses his body. If you touch the shoulders of your ten-year-old boy, you will often find that his muscles are rock hard with tension.

Then, one day, puberty strikes. The boy is suddenly aware of a wonderful feeling of aliveness, of quickening, all located in one place! It's no wonder a boy soon attaches all his feelings of closeness (and all his sense of aliveness and well-being) to the activities of his penis.

Boys want to feel alive in their bodies. That's why they like music with a heavy beat, and why they love activity, speed, and danger. They instinctively know this can help them break into manhood. A boy who enjoys his body and can hug his mom, dad, and siblings, often has many ways to feel good—dancing, drumming, or playing sports for the buzz of the game itself. For these boys, sex carries a little less weight—it's a pleasure, rather than an obsession.

Keeping Things Open and Positive

Parents must be careful not to drive sexuality underground by ridiculing their son about sex or girls. Do talk about it when it comes up in movies or TV or discussions at the table. As boys pass the age of ten, use sexual words casually and normally in conversation—*masturbation, lovemaking, orgasm*—as well as the darker ones, such as *rape* and *incest*. They need to know that you know about these aspects of life. But be particularly open about sex as a lovely and exciting aspect of life.

Demand maturity—with good humor. If you notice your sons sniggering or reacting in a silly way to an incident on TV or in the conversation, don't just let it go—ask them about it, and fill out their understanding. But end with a joke or a laugh. Give things a more positive spin. The antidote to "creepiness" is an infusion of warmth, humor, and openness.

Mothers can really help here. If a mother is affectionate and praises her son's attractiveness (without flirting with him), and if a father shows respect for the mother (and

PRACTICAL HELP

Boys Who Want to Be Girls

A frequent question from parents is about sons who like to dress up as girls or even say they want to be a girl. Alison Soutter, a psychologist with the NSW Department of School Education, carried out a fifteen-year study of three boys in the UK who were diagnosed with "gender identity disorder"—and the news is good.

Soutter believes that the wish to be a girl—to dress like a girl and carry out what are normally seen as "girls'" activities—is quite common among boys. She sees it as a delay in development—not a fixed problem—and one that parents can best handle with tolerance and some help in avoiding teasing. It is not connected with homosexuality, and the boys she studied outgrew the "disorder" by late adolescence.

For a boy to want to be a girl goes against a lot of peer pressure, so it must be quite a strong wish. To suppress this wish seems cruel and likely to cause a lot of tension in the child. In fact, when Alison Soutter went on British radio to talk about her study, a number of transvestite men (men who dress as women) phoned in to say that when they were young, they were prevented from dressing as girls and this just made them more determined. It's likely that this opposition led them to becoming fixated as adults on cross-dressing.

Because teasing is such a painful experience and can lead to many other problems, boys with genuine gender identity disorder need help and protection from hurtful actions. For instance, a more "alternative" school, with more acceptance and tolerance of differences, would be far preferable to a conformist school or one where there is a lot of bullying. Strategies for self-protection from teasing are also important for the boys to learn.

Alison Soutter is unsure about causation, but the three boys in her study all had fathers who had disabilities or illnesses that kept them in a passive position within the family. It may be that the good, warm involvement of a father in family life works preventively, ensuring that boys find the male role more appealing.

expresses his attraction in a positive and nonsleazy way), then the boy learns how to relate to girls with attraction and *equality*. If boys and girls are encouraged in school or youth groups to talk and mix and have friendships that are not "dates," they can learn more about the opposite sex without the self-consciousness of "going steady." They can graduate in friendship first and major in romance later.

Tenderness Is Taught

In the 1960s, anthropologist James Prescott carried out a large study of child-rearing and violence across different societies. He found that those societies that gave less touching and affection to young children had by far the most violence among adults. It's clear that the more tenderness and warmth children experience, the safer and more loving they will be as adults. Treating children with warmth and affection helps immunize them against the wish or need to harm others.

Your Son and Online Porn

When we were teenagers, serious pornography was almost unheard of. Of course, most boys managed to garner a small stash of magazines showing almost-nude young women, who were usually referred to in the magazines as "co-eds," possibly to emphasize their educational status. Otherwise, the renowned poster of Raquel Welch in a rabbit-fur bikini from the film *One Million Years B.C.* graced some bedroom walls, and that was it. Parents either didn't notice or didn't think it worth commenting on. As a psychologist I would have regarded this—the boys' interest and their parents' non-interference—as healthy and normal, as long as it was discreet and private, like sex itself. Respectful boundaries are important in how we treat each other, especially in those parts of life that involve emotional closeness and vulnerability.

The rise of online pornography has blown all this out of the water. Today's mental-health professionals and law-enforcement authorities are alarmed and are rushing to find a balanced reaction. Parents need to know about this, as the harm to boys' minds is becoming very clear. In 2012, the renowned Tavistock Clinic in London sounded an alarm to parents everywhere by speaking out about the rise in cases of young boys experiencing addiction to hard-core porn online. One boy who had started at ten years of age told a counselor, "I didn't know it was possible for people to do those sort of things. The websites led me to other websites, and soon I was looking at weirder stuff I could never have imagined—animals, children, stabbing and strangling." For three years, unknown to his parents, this boy viewed porn for hours every night. He is still deeply disturbed by its effects on him. He told the counselor, "It still makes me think I might never have a proper girlfriend—the pictures still come back to me sometimes. It makes me want to shout Stop, stop!'"

Online porn addiction has spilled over into rapes and assaults in the real world. Among the Tavistock's patients was a thirteen-year-old who was found to have been abusing his five-year-old sister. A twelve-year-old was exposing himself to teachers and other students at school. Therapist John Woods told the UK's *Daily Mail* newspaper that for every child who comes to the attention of police or counselors, there are thousands nobody yet knows about.

A UK parliamentary report in 2012 found that a shocking 80 percent of sixteen-year-old boys regularly access porn online. And one in three ten-year-olds has seen explicit material. It's these younger boys who are the most concern, because their sexuality is still being formed and can easily be molded toward cruelty and non-intimate sex. One does have to ask, what were these boys' parents doing—didn't they know about their sons' online behavior?

Researchers have found that the more that porn is viewed by boys or men, the more those males denigrate and dehumanize women—they lose respect for them as people. And they see them as deserving of maltreatment. Also, the nature of solitary sexuality has changed: what once satisfied is now not enough, and the viewer seeks stronger material. Porn sites are designed to entrap, sometimes even using children's cartoon characters or placement among game sites to get children to click through.

Neuropsychologist Susan Greenfield has written extensively about how the Internet shapes brains and makes instant gratification an addiction in itself. Boys who get addicted to online porn often spend hours a day (and night) trawling the Internet when they are supposed to be asleep or doing their homework. Many tell counselors they now find real girls too difficult to relate to—they prefer "sex" online.

Given the proliferation of smartphones and wireless devices with Internet connections, your son is likely to be shown things by friends. Difficult as you may find it, it's important to talk calmly and reasonably about this: that there is weird pornography about, that it's harmful to keep looking at, and that you want him not to do that. (It's ongoing exposure that you really want to prevent.) Have filters on your computer(s), and only have computer access in public parts of your house, not in bedrooms. If your kids have smartphones, don't let them keep them overnight—leave them all on chargers in the kitchen. Don't make your son feel bad for being curious about or attracted to pictures of women—that's totally normal. But explain that you do want to guard him against getting addicted. Porn is very tempting, and some of his peers will probably urge him to "look at this." A boy who can say, "No thanks, that stuff messes with your head," is going to be the one who finds that his real-life relationships are a whole lot better and happier.

Finally, just as we have laws to restrict kids' access to other harmful things, like alcohol and tobacco, making Internet service providers restrict pornography, so that it can't be accessed without deliberate and identified actions, is essential. Pornography is a bigger industry than sport, worth billions of dollars, so it's a powerful lobby group. Taming it will take some real resolve.

Some Practicalities: Masturbation and Pornography

Scottish comedian Billy Connolly became famous for tackling taboo topics long before others were game. He says the following about masturbation:

"The one advantage masturbation has over sex is that you don't have to look your best . . . I remember my first sexual experience as a very frightening experience—it was dark and I was alone!"

All males masturbate—in their teens, during marriage, and in old age. It's a simple mechanism for keeping sperm renewed and letting off steam. But it's something more than this. Just as lovemaking is so much more than just a physical thing, so masturbation is a way that young people get to feel good and learn about their bodies. Orgasm (experienced without guilt in a relaxed and trusting state of mind) is really a spiritual experience. For a few seconds your body is lost in the stars and nature's rhythms take over—and all just an arm's length away!

Parents need only do two things:

1. Let boys know masturbation is okay.

2. Respect the privacy of boys' bedrooms after lights out—and ask that they use tissues to avoid gumming up acres of sheets, pajamas, and pillowcases!

Pornography is a slightly more complicated question. A father once asked me: "My son is fourteen. He has pictures of naked women all over his bedroom walls. Is this okay?" (I love these questions!)

SB: "How do you feel about it?"

Him: "I'm not real comfortable about it."

SB: "And your wife—how does she feel?"

Him: "She hates them."

SB: "Uh-huh. I think both of your feelings are important to listen to. It isn't wrong for women to show their bodies, or for boys to be interested in looking at them or fantasizing about them. What's a problem is where and when and with whom. If a boy has magazines, he should keep them privately to himself. His mother and sisters shouldn't have to see the pictures glaring out. And if his mother objects to him even owning them, that is fine. A father should support her in this."

I posed this question on a fathers' Internet chat group, and there were some wonderful replies. Most men remembered hoarding pictures or magazines when they were about this age. But they also noted that the pictures were far less explicit than they are now, and not as readily available. Far more was left to the imagination.

The age of the boy made a big difference. Most fathers took a totally different view about boys under thirteen or so having access to sexually posed pictures of women. They felt that it prematurely sexualized the boys and got in the way of the *real* goal at this age, which was for them to have friendships with girls without being hung up about sex (for which they were not emotionally or physically ready).

One man wrote: "I would ask a fourteen-year-old to hide his magazines and keep them out of sight, or I would have to take them. But with a nine-year-old I would take them away and toss them out—and have a talk with him about why."

Inevitably, boys will see these images in magazines passed among friends or on the Internet. What is needed is close enough monitoring by parents so that you are able to prevent really objectionable material from circulating among boys, while at the same time not shaming the boys for being interested or curious.

Erotica can have an educational role, and boys' curiosity is healthy and natural. The bestseller *The Joy of Sex* succeeded because it was the first mass-market publication with images that were tasteful, erotic, and quite tender.

Drawings also do not involve trading in real human beings, which is the saddest aspect of photographic porn.

When boys do see these images, you can help them to think about the messages the pictures send, why they are sold, what is portrayed, and whether or not they are respectful of women. (Some pictures are and some are not.) Fathers or mothers may well help their sons find better erotica to look at and read. It's a delicate but not impossible area to navigate. Keep your sense of humor handy.

What we want our boys to think when they see an attractive woman is that she is attractive *and* a person with feelings. Pornography takes away the personhood of women.

Parents must also teach daughters not to misuse their physical appeal to exploit or tease boys—creepiness can work both ways. Sex is about mutual respect and mutual enjoyment. It's a part of loving, and not a marketing tool.

If Your Son Is Gay

Parenthood is rather strange. Most of us have a fantasy family long before we have a real one. Even before our children are born, we have their lives mapped out for them! And what conservative dreams they usually are—a career, marriage, and grandchildren to sit on our knee. Finding out that your teenage son is gay demolishes several of these fond hopes and replaces them with scary images instead. It's natural to feel some grief and concern.

Part of the problem is the stereotypes. Although Gay Pride parades have done great things for gay pride, they haven't helped the fantasies of moms and dads in the suburbs! And they are hardly a realistic depiction of the full spectrum of gay life.

When it's all boiled down, the concerns of parents of a gay son are just the same as those of any parent. You want your son to have a happy life. You hope that he will handle his sexuality in a responsible and self-respecting way. And you hope that he will not move away into worlds that are beyond your reach or understanding.

Gay teenagers need our support. There is no doubt they are at risk—from our rejection and from a harsh world. It's now believed that many youth suicides are actually carried out by youngsters who discover they are gay and perceive, rightly or wrongly, that dealing with this in their family or community might be unbearably difficult. Gay kids need parents who will listen and understand—and protect them from harassment or persecution.

It's not very fruitful to dwell on "why?" or "where did we go wrong?" Evidence is mounting that some babies are born

with certain hormonal settings from early in the womb, which may set the brain as either gay, bisexual, or heterosexual. (At least one in ten young men is gay or bisexual.)

Sometimes family dynamics play a part—certainly some gay men had remote and critical fathers, and are seeking fatherly affection from a gay lover. But this alone isn't enough to determine sexual orientation. Trying to talk a young man out of being gay just makes him feel more rejected and more desperate.

Like any community, the gay community certainly has its sleazy side, often created by loneliness and rejection, and sometimes the very real need to conceal one's sexual orientation and activity to protect one's personal safety and livelihood. But if you love and support your son, he will be less likely to drop into self-loathing or despair, and more likely to be self-respecting and careful about safe sex, for example. There are countless numbers of happy and successful gay men and women. Life will be better for gay teenagers when gay adults are more visible. Perhaps one day schools will intentionally have some gay staff members so that children will see that normal, caring, and happy people can be lesbian or gay.

If you're a parent of a gay son, it's a good idea to desensitize yourself and learn what you can. An excellent Australian movie with Jack Thompson, *The Sum of Us*, looks at a father's attitude toward his son's homosexuality and is very positive.

The hardest thing about having a gay son can be the way it isolates you—you feel different from other parents. Talking to other parents of gay offspring is the very best thing you can do. (Groups such as PFLAG—Parents and Friends of Lesbians and Gays—exist worldwide and offer support.) A gay son can take you into a world of interesting and wonderful people!

In a Nutshell

1. Teach boys the differences between liking, loving, and lusting. All are okay, but you shouldn't mix them up.

2. Have a small rite of passage at age ten and give them some positive messages about sex.

3. Guard against creepiness by teaching your sons to be respectful of all people. Help them find settings and activities that give them a chance know girls as friends.

4. Discourage the trend to sexualize boy-girl relationships under sixteen years of age.

5. Remember that boys, too, want to be loved, not just "sexed." Affirm and support their romantic side.

6. Help them keep their bodies alive through dance, drumming, music, massage, and so on. Continue to hug and show affection to your sons as long as they are comfortable with it.

7. Tenderness is learned by receiving it—from babyhood onward. The real lessons about relationships are learned by age three.

8. Masturbation isn't just harmless—it's good for you.

9. Discourage pornography; discuss it and its messages. Don't shame a boy for his interest, but talk about what makes good erotica—respectful, happy, involving relationships. And perhaps help him find some.

10. Mothers can help sons understand what girls like in young men—kindness, conversation, and a sense of fun.

11. Gay sons need understanding, and for their parents to accept them and get to better know their world.

CHAPTER EIGHT

A Revolution in Schooling

Many schools today are a battleground. Teachers are over-stressed and underpaid; kids have less and less socialization from home (good manners, calm influences, feeling wanted and loved). The number of men in schools has plummeted. More and more, it is women who have to deal with physically intimidating and disrespectful boys. The classroom becomes a battleground for survival with only two goals—getting the girls to achieve and getting the boys to behave.

So boys create stress, but they themselves are suffering, too. Girls outperform boys in almost every subject. Something has to be done about boys' motivation, for everyone's sake.

From what we have already described here about brain differences, hormones, and the need for male role models, it's clear that schools can and must change if they are to become good places for boys. The following are some starting points.

A Later Starting Age for Boys

The slower development of boys' fine-motor skills, and their cognitive skills in general, suggests that many boys would benefit by starting school a year later—and therefore moving through school a year after girls of the same age. This is especially true of boys who are young for their intake year. Some very bright and able boys (like Einstein, for example) were very slow starters.

Each child deserves equal consideration based on some simple screening of fine-motor skills and in consultation with parents and a preschool teacher. Ideally, every child of four should attend half-day preschool, where school readiness is easy to judge. Many schools today have to dissuade parents who see education as a race and who wish to enroll children earlier and earlier, as if they can get a head start!

Thoughtful parents will understand the benefits of a delayed start for boys, once they are explained. Since birthdays fall all through the year, the starting age is already a matter of some flexibility, and this can be made more flexible based on actual ability—a far more rational approach. Some slower developing girls may also benefit from a year's delay.

More Men in School, of the Right Kind

Because of divorce and single motherhood, up to a third of boys have no father present at home. The six-to-fourteen age range is the period when boys most hunger for male encouragement and example. So it's vital that we get more men into primary school teaching. But not just any men—they have to be the right kind of men.

I have asked many teachers to describe the right kind of man to work with boys. Two qualities come up again and again:

1. A mixture of warmth and sternness. Someone who obviously enjoys youngsters and gives praise where it is due. A man who doesn't need to be "one of the boys" but has a slightly gruff, no-nonsense manner. This means that order prevails, and boys can get on with the work, excursion, sports, or whatever. But he must have warmth and a sense of humor.

2. Lack of defensiveness. A man who is not only in charge, but also shows it in a way that doesn't issue a challenge

to every testosterone-boosted boy in the room. He doesn't need to prove anything and doesn't feel threatened by youthful exuberance.

Discipline Problems Call for Our Involvement

Boys make trouble to get noticed. In schools all around the world where I have consulted, there is a proven equation: an under-fathered boy equals a discipline problem in school. Under-fathered boys unconsciously want men to address the problems in their lives, but don't know how to ask for help. Girls *ask* for help; boys often just *act* for help.

If we get male teachers involved with under-fathered boys (ideally before they make trouble), we can turn their lives around. And if boys do get into trouble, male teachers should work with them to guide and help them.

Recent studies have found that boys in school who act as if they don't care, really *do* want to be successful and included. We have just made the slope too steep for them. We punish them, but we don't offer leadership.

Leadership is not just something that comes from the podium at assembly. It has to be personal.

Too often boys' vitality is seen as a threat, something to be squashed. The squashing was once done by corporal punishment and grinding work. Now suspensions or time-out rooms or tedious and bureaucratic "report" systems do the job. One teacher described to me his school's disciplinary report system as "lingering, inconclusive, and impersonal." This is all based on a psychology of distance, not closeness: "If you're bad, we'll isolate you." It should be: "If you need help that badly, we'll get involved with you." School should be a place of affection, involvement, and attachment. The more needy the boy is, the more he receives.

Education with Energy

The learning environment of schools seems designed to educate senior citizens, not young people at their most energetic. Everyone is supposed to be quiet, nice, and compliant. Excitement has no place in this kind of learning environment (though many wonderful teachers do manage to bring some fun and energy into their classes, and many children catch this spirit and run with it).

School-required passivity contradicts everything we know about kids, especially adolescents. Adolescence is the age of passion. Boys (and girls) crave an engaged and intense learning experience, with men and women who challenge them and get to know them personally—and from this specific knowledge of their needs, work with them to shape and extend their intellect, spirit, and skills. If kids aren't waking up in the morning saying, "Wow! School today!" something is not right.

Some kids are more passionate than others. Their specific passions and talents (not just their testosterone levels) make certain kids itch to do something of significance, something real and socially useful, or something really creative. If this vitality is not engaged, then it turns into misbehavior and troublemaking.

The passion in the child has to be matched with an equal investment from the parents, teachers, or other mentors. The old initiators weren't casual or laid-back—they took boys into the desert and taught them one-on-one about life-and-death concerns. Their graduation ceremonies were powerful and significant events for the young men. In other cultures, boys would dance nonstop all night or walk 180 miles to fetch material for their initiation. These societies understood something about the energies of adolescence.

The Principal Is the Key

A male principal or senior teacher is an important, symbolic figure in children's minds— something between a father substitute and a god substitute! Knowing this, he must make it his business to know the kids, especially the high-risk boys and girls, long before they get into trouble. Then, if there's a problem, the relationship is already established and it's easier to talk things through.

A principal is also the key to getting boys to take on leadership, which these days they commonly reject. Australian school principal Peter Ireland wrote in *Boys in Schools* about a strategy that he implemented. Peter began regular schoolyard meetings with selected boys to build up their sense of belonging and participation in the life of the school. The meetings focused on understanding the boys' view of school, the impediments to their involvement, and how to solve these. The boys who participated in these meetings became significantly more involved in both their own studies and the community life of the school. They just needed encouragement.

Helping Boys with Their Vulnerable Areas

Language and expression are two specific weak areas for boys. As we've explained earlier, boys' brains are wired in a way that makes it harder for them to take feelings and impressions from the right side of their brain and put these into words on the left side. They need extra help to master written language, express themselves verbally, and learn to enjoy reading. They have a right to this help under any concept of equity in schooling. Special programs for boys in English, reading, and drama are urgently needed from kindergarten upward. Here is how one school tackled this problem, with spectacular results.

PRACTICAL HELP

The Cotswold Experiment

Two big debates keep rearing their heads in the world of education, even making it onto the front pages of the newspapers.

The first is about single-sex schools versus coeducation. Are boys and girls better off separated? Boys not only do poorly at school, but also their behavior often prevents girls and quieter boys from learning. Parents of girls solve the problem by enrolling their daughters in girls-only schools. But where can the boys run to?

The second debate is about the decline in boys' accomplishment and participation at school, which has been noted in most industrial countries. Boys are doing poorly in relation to girls, especially in subjects like English, art, the humanities, and languages.

This problem tested the mind of Marion Cox, head of English at the Cotswold School, a coeducational secondary school in the countryside of Leicestershire in England. Marion decided to conduct an experiment. She assigned boys and girls in the fourth year of secondary school to gender-segregated English classes, where they remained for two years. (In all other subjects, they still studied together in the conventional way.)

As the new, single-sex classes got under way, teachers adjusted the curriculum (that is, the choice of books and poems) to make it more interesting for the boys or girls in their class. They were no longer restricted by trying to strike a middle path between the interests of boys and girls. The classes started to take on a distinctly boys' or girls' flavor.

Class sizes were kept to about twenty-one students—smaller than the average before the study. In addition, teachers introduced some intensive writing and reading support (encouragement and supervision to read during class time) for the boys.

The Results?

The results were impressive. According to national statistics for the United Kingdom, only 9 percent of fourteen-year-old boys nationwide achieve grades in the range of A to C for English. (English is not a subject that most boys either like or do well in!) In the Cotswold School, following two years of the new separate classes, 34 percent of boys scored in the A to C range in their final exams. *The school had increased the number of boys in the high-scoring range by almost 400 percent.*

And the girls did better, too. An impressive 75 percent of girls got scores in the A to C range compared with 46 percent the previous year. (Note that the girls' results were still dramatically higher than the boys'!)

The gender separation effects have caused considerable excitement around the UK. Marion Cox told the *Times* newspaper that the benefits went far beyond just English scores. "Behavior, concentration, and reading levels all improved significantly. I believe if we can catch them even younger than fourteen, before they give up books for TV and the computer, and the antiheroic role models are entrenched, we would have even better chances of success."

A Good Alternative to Single-Sex Schools

When I spoke to Marion Cox by phone, she explained that boys at the school found that they could relax and express themselves more without girls present, and girls reported the same. She felt that separation "just for English" was a good alternative to the more extreme solution of single-sex schools. Marion noted, "The most frequent observation from visitors to our classes was that the atmosphere was more calm and settled. Boys were learning to enjoy reading—often for the first time."

The Cotswold experiment did two things:

- It acknowledged that boys generally have a slower acquisition of language skills and helped them with this.

- It gave boys a safe environment where they wouldn't feel stupid in front of the girls, who were so much more articulate. The boys didn't have to "act up" to cover up their inadequacies, and they began to take risks by reading and writing poetry, acting in plays, and so on.

Essential Skills for Boys

Skills in English are vital to life. The abilities to reason and communicate with language are what make you a good parent, partner, and workmate. Self-expression is also the way out of the terrible emotional isolation that some boys and men feel, which may lead to alcoholism, domestic violence, or even suicide.

Segregating classes and the curriculum is not risk-free. There is always a danger of reintroducing stereotypes: boys study war; girls study love! A lot depends on the teacher's attitude. The Cotswold results are encouraging: when separated, the girls and boys seemed able to relax and drop the old roles. The boys became more expressive and open, the girls more assertive. It seems to be an approach where everybody wins.

Helping Boys Helps Girls, Too

Thinking about boys' needs sometimes worries those who have worked hard to raise girls' attainment. They fear that girls might be pushed back into the old box. My experience is that nothing is going to stop girls now, though of course we must still be active and organized in helping them, as new assaults on girlhood come from the media and the failure of some parents to really help and support them.

But one of the greatest needs girls have is for boys to change. To create a good learning environment and a safe world, girls' and boys' needs are deeply intertwined.

The boys-versus-girls debate is quite unnecessary. What the Cotswold experiment (see page 154) shows is that everyone can benefit if we tailor programs to each special-needs group in the school. Boys, girls, low-income groups, ethnic groups, and so on all present different challenges. Everyone is human, everyone is special, and everyone deserves to be treated according to his or her individual needs. This is the way forward for schooling.

STORIES FROM THE HEART

Homework Hell

Every time I talk to parents, someone asks about how to choose a school for their son. The guidelines at the end of this book are a big help with this, but there is another factor. Often the best-equipped and most prestigious schools are also the unhappiest. It can be summed up in one word. *Pressure*. Pressure of a kind that actually destroys kids' love of learning. And this is nowhere more obvious than in the scourge of homework. Many psychologists and counselors now believe homework, beyond some simple reviewing of the daily concepts learned, does more harm than good. Let this letter that a distressed, yet very articulate, mother sent to me explain why.

Dear Steve,

My son's school is potentially a wonderful school. It has a wealth of facilities, labs, art rooms, auditoriums, sports fields, and so on. It has some exceptional teachers. Boys at the school are winning sporting events, gaining high marks, achieving excellence in music, art, and drama.

However, there is something insidious happening at the school, which causes many boys great distress and turns others away from academic pursuits for life. A misdirected emphasis, an imbalance. I refer of course to the academic pressure, and one manifestation—homework.

The school resolutely demands that boys from the age of eight years onward complete an extremely heavy homework load every night regardless of everything else that is happening in the boy's (and his family's) life. It's so depressing for a parent to hear a boy say he has "heaps" of homework, and see him dejected and tired instead of happy to face an evening at home. It is devastating to see a fourteen-year-old boy (who has grown an inch in the last ten weeks) trudge home and tearfully say he just can't do any homework tonight. He falls asleep in his clothes, knowing he will have drills and detentions the following day. Are the expectations productive? Would one hour's homework a night give the same standardized test result as three hours?

Parents end up supervising and harassing boys who work before dinner and into the night. Surely it is more logical to set a small amount of homework and teach boys to work on their own. Self-motivated work must be more valuable than work completed in anger and frustration. But will the boy who has tried against all the odds to achieve the three hours of compulsory homework a night give up, lose himself in despair, and vow to never pursue a career with university requirements? Worst of all, will he abhor intellectual inquiry ever after?

There are other negative effects that homework has, not only on the boy but on his home, too. A boy gets up at 6:30 to leave home by 7:30 for school, and three out of four afternoons gets home at 6:00 or 6:30. He has to have time for dinner. Then it is homework. Shouldn't a boy be expected to take some responsibility for the smooth running of the household in which he lives? But when? It is the mothers who pick up the pieces when the boy is in despair of ever achieving the expectations set. The school is setting a blueprint for many boys—that they will never achieve reward for their effort—and expecting families to wait on boys, with clothes, meals, and transport, all to support the superhuman study effort. This conditions boys to expect the same from their spouses—which in the twenty-first century is not going to happen.

It would be to the school's credit if it could take a lead and stand above the destructive values that society has adopted. Take a stand by saying that music is for pleasure and sports are for fun—and that is what this school will teach its boys, so that as adults they will still be playing their musical instruments, still be playing their chosen sports, still debating, still acting in plays, because school made it fun and something they want to take into their adult lives.

Has my son's school got the guts to take a stand? I don't think so.

Marian

Bullying

Being physically intimidated, hit, hurt, or humiliated by other larger children happens too often in our schools and communities. It adds to the perception that the United States is a violent country, where no one can feel safe.

In fact, childhood violence is at the root of wider violence, and it's here that it has to be stopped. We need no greater reminder of this than the sad fact that 250 students have been killed in American schools in the past twelve years, and most of the Columbine-style mass shootings have been conducted by boys who were relentlessly bullied before finally taking carefully planned revenge.

According to the largest study across the country, one in six children report being frequently bullied. Also, it has been discovered that teachers underestimate by a factor of three the actual incidence of bullying in schools.

Luckily, attention is now being paid to this huge and disabling problem that stops boys (and girls, too) from going about their lives happily and safely. We know how to stop bullying in schools, and no student should have to tolerate ongoing bullying. If they do, schools are not doing their jobs.

What causes bullying? Part of the problem is competitiveness and academic difficulties when not all boys are helped to learn. Less able students feel excluded and resentful, and use physical means to regain some of their self-esteem and dignity. One leading expert, Dr. Ken Rigby, believes bullying is worst where schools themselves bully students, belittling them and making them feel useless, and not helping them to find ways to learn and succeed.

My belief is that violent bullies are often hit a lot at home and have lost a child's natural reluctance to hurt others. They do to others what was done to them. Thirty percent of children who are bullies report also being bullied by others. Bullying is linked to a bygone era when men hit their wives routinely, and wives and husbands hit children. Thankfully, family violence is less and less accepted today.

Programs to end bullying are now being implemented in many American schools with considerable success. The most successful programs include a multi-pronged approach:

1. Increase the knowledge of staff and students about bullying through seminars, lessons, and discussions so the problem is out in the open and continually being studied and evaluated.

2. Implement a consistent system of school-wide intervention and follow-up to bullying incidents, so everyone knows what to do, and this becomes normal and accepted.

3. Teach protective skills to students and empower them to deal with bullying situations, but emphasize and guarantee that when this is not enough, adults will offer help and take action.

4. Form a mobilized and caring community among the 80 percent of students who are neither bullies nor victims, but who can act to look out for and stick up for the others. This additional element may be the greatest key; almost all bullying has witnesses and depends on the complicity of witnesses. Once this norm is changed, bullying cannot thrive.

PRACTICAL HELP

How to Spot an Under-Fathered Boy in School

There are four main clues that a boy is seriously under-fathered:

- An aggressive style of relating
- Hyper-masculine behavior and interests (guns, muscles, monster trucks, death)
- Extremely limited repertoire of behavior (standing around grunting and being "cool")
- Derogatory attitude toward women, gays, and minorities

These traits are familiar to every secondary school teacher in the Western world. Let's examine what is causing them.

The aggressive style of relating is a boy's cover-up for feeling unsure of himself. Lacking praise and respect from older males, he puts on a tough act. The rule is, put down someone else before he puts you down. If a boy has little contact with his father or other men, then he doesn't really know how to be a man. He doesn't have the words, the insights into himself, or a handle on his feelings. Because he's never seen it done, he doesn't know how to:

- Deal with a conflict in a good-humored way
- Talk to women easily and without being sexist
- Express appreciation or sadness, or to say sorry and so on

A boy like this has only two sources from which to draw his image of masculinity—men in the movies (and on TV, the Internet, video games) and his own peer group. If his hero is Jean-Claude Van Damme, he may not get a lot of help from this in handling real life. And his peer group is as lost as he is—capable only of grunts and one-word exclamations like "Yo."

My memory of boyhood, echoed by that of many men I talk to, is of considerable fear of being ridiculed or beaten up by other boys. Boys dread ridicule—however tough they act. They often feel deeply ashamed of their slowness when reading aloud or looking dumb in the classroom. They dread being shown up by a teacher. Boys who are smart have the opposite problem—being called a nerd or a teacher's pet and also facing ridicule or exclusion. If you are creative or different, you run the risk of being teased as well.

The boy with good support from his father and mother, uncles, and so on can handle this better because he doesn't feel that his maleness is on trial. But a boy who doesn't feel assured of his masculinity has to cover up. The best protection is to act tough and uncaring and radiate aggression, so that nobody thinks you're scared. You get in first and put people down as a matter of course. This way, you feel safer.

The same effect takes place with interests. A tough dude has to have tough interests. Boys (not having the perspective of a real man around to broaden their interests with hobbies, sports, or music, or to involve them in creative work in a shed or garden) gravitate to those things that make them feel masculine—action figures with huge muscles, guns, trucks, and so on.

Praise Is the Antidote

If a father, uncle, or older friend praises a boy, this automatically widens that boy's self-image. Imagine the family is coming home from a barbecue with friends. The dad says casually, "You were really good with the little kids, organizing that soccer game. They loved it!" The boy drinks this compliment in deep. (His mother could have said the same thing, but in the teens this would not have gone in so deeply.)

A male teacher or a friend sees the boy tapping on the table in a complex rhythm: "You know, you could be a drummer—that's a really hard rhythm." Such a comment boosts the boy's sense of himself. He is less dependent on peer approval and more willing to take risks.

What Are You, a Girl?

If you don't know what you are, then there is one way to firm up your self-image—by declaring what you are not. Dr. Rex Stoessiger has noticed in his work on boys' literacy that boys who don't have a positive male image define themselves by being *not girls*. So they are not everything that they perceive girls to be—soft, talkative, emotional, cooperative, caring, and affectionate. They reject every soft quality, and they reject girls, too. Having someone to hate and reject makes them feel stronger, more worthy.

Boys' self-esteem is thus the key to ending a lot of racism and sexism, which are significant social problems today.

Role Models, Good and Bad

A teacher I was talking to recently illustrated the effect of role-modeling beautifully. In the large country high school where she taught, the normally girl-dominated subject of art had recently become a popular choice for boys, because the new art teacher

was a man with a good-hearted personality. A father with kids of his own, he was warm, positive, and a bit stern. He had interests that the kids respected. He organized school surfing competitions, was an avid surfer, and liked the outdoors. The result: a sudden upsurge of boys' painting, sculpture, and creativity, which lasted several years after this man left the school.

5. Get individualized help and family intervention and follow-up for persistently violent children. Violent children become violent adults unless significant help is offered to turn this around.

Whole school community approaches, especially discussions and interventions at the classroom level, mean that the problem isn't driven underground and that bullies themselves experience some understanding and help, along with zero tolerance of their behavior. Through this concerted approach—role plays, discussion, the supportive and positive presence of teachers in the playground, and no more copping out or discounting the seriousness of bullying on the school's part—a significant change can be made. A whole school's climate of caring and learning can be reformed. Bullying is a core symptom of a dysfunctional school and should be the first thing a

parent seeks assurance about in choosing a school. Scared children can't learn.

WHAT PARENTS CAN DO

For parents, the following indicators are warning signs that your child may be getting bullied:

- Physical signs (unexplained bruises, scratches, cuts, or damage to clothes or belongings)
- Stress-caused illnesses (pains, headaches, and stomachaches that seem unexplained)
- Fearful behavior (fear of walking to school, going different routes, asking to be driven)
- Dropping off in quality of schoolwork
- Coming home hungry (perhaps lunch or lunch money is being stolen)
- Asking for or stealing money (to pay the bully)
- Having few friends
- Rarely being invited to parties
- Changes in behavior (withdrawal, stammering, moodiness, irritability, appearing upset, unhappy, tearful, or distressed)
- Not eating
- Anxiety (shown by bed-wetting, nail-biting, fearfulness, tics, not sleeping, or crying out in sleep)
- Refusal to say what is wrong
- At the worst extreme, hinting at suicide or actually attempting suicide
- Giving improbable excuses for any of the above

Of course, there are other possible reasons for many of these symptoms, and you should also get a doctor to check that those physical symptoms do not have another cause. A good doctor can also gently question your child to find out about bullying.

Although the listed symptoms may sound somewhat obvious, the fact is that boys often won't talk about bullying in the first place because it seems weak to do so. Also, they may have been threatened with consequences if they tell, or they may fear it will make things worse to speak up.

If your child is being bullied, talk to the school. Take along written details of what has happened to your child, and calmly express your concerns. Expect that two or even three meetings may be necessary to give the school time to investigate and decide what to do. Don't just hand off your list and leave them to deal with it. It will have to be a joint effort. Either you or a school counselor can also work with your child to practice assertiveness, giving humorous replies to name-calling, telling bullies, "Leave me alone, I don't like it," and acting and sounding determined. In primary school, a boy who knows how to make friends and avoid trouble, and who can speak up for himself, generally is ignored by bullies. Rigby and Slee recommend martial-arts training as a way to build physical confidence and assertiveness for children who are getting victimized a lot.

Avoid schools that are too big and impersonal. The limits to what can function as a caring community are about four hundred pupils in a primary school and six hundred in a secondary school. Anything larger will often become an inefficient education "factory." Kids will join gangs for self-protection, and bullying is a natural side effect of gangs.

Schools that are less competitively based, such as Waldorf and other alternative schools, generally have a more caring atmosphere in which children and teachers are closer and more involved, and bullying is uncommon. A very gentle child may benefit from a move to such a school.

Almost every child, boy or girl, will experience bullying and, if helped to acquire assertiveness skills, will overcome it. Most schools around the country are introducing the methods described here, but perhaps yours needs some encouragement. All of us—families, schools, and society—need to learn to live without intimidation of each other.

Role-Modeling Is How Humans Learn

The role-model concept cannot be overemphasized—it keeps cropping up with every teacher we talk to. Role-modeling is an evolutionary trait in humans. We are a species that has few instincts and must learn complex skills to survive. By watching a person we admire in action, our brain takes in a cluster of skills, attitudes, and values. We don't need our role models to be great heroes—in some ways it's preferable to simply have people who are accessible and whom we like. An adolescent is a role-seeking missile, and he or she will lock on to a range of targets before downloading enough material to shape a personal identity.

A role model has to be seen by the teenager as "someone like me" or "someone I could be like." Girls need role models at least as much as boys do, but girls get far more role models in school, and those female teachers often seem to share more of themselves. Consequently, girls take in far more data on how to be a woman than boys do on how to be a man.

Role models can be surprising and diverse. They must also challenge and stretch youngsters' ideas. In the fairly impoverished outer suburban high school I attended in the 1960s, I can remember some men who were positive gems:

- A math teacher who was also our home-group teacher and visited every child's parents at home (causing a spate of renovation and new furniture purchases through the year). The purpose of the visits was to persuade parents to let us stay at school for longer (at a time when staying on until finishing high school was seen as a pretty ambitious thing to do). Although quite a slave driver in the classroom, this man also took us on the first long school excursion ever—a wonderful experience. He later became a well-known professor of education.
- An elderly man, an old soldier who cycled to work, who taught us to love poetry. He inflicted Shakespeare on us even though it wasn't in the curriculum, but also took us exploring in nature, taught yoga, and gave up many weekends to take us on hikes and campouts.
- A radical communist English teacher, who warned us about the escalating Vietnam war, told us about social advances in Russia, and got us to read *To Kill a Mockingbird* and *Shane*.
- An electronics whiz who spent lunchtimes with kids who wanted to make and mend radios.

With all of these role models, along with cheerful sports teachers and plenty of great female teachers, school really did broaden our horizons on what being male could be about.

What Are "Learning Difficulties"?

Almost everyone has some brain damage. Small amounts of damage may take place at birth or be caused by blows to the head, genetic impairment, mercury or lead in the environment, or one's parents smoking or drinking during pregnancy. Boys are more prone to brain damage, though the reasons for this are not well understood.

Minor brain damage isn't a problem, unless your child has some trouble with learning. In the past, many learning problems passed unnoticed because high levels of literacy were less important. Today the same problems can be a real disadvantage—but luckily a lot can be done to help.

There are four main types of learning difficulties, relating to the way information is processed. For a child to learn, information has to do four things: it has to go into his brain through his sensory nerves, get organized to make sense, be kept there in memory, and then be brought out again when needed.

1. **Input** This might mean hearing a teacher properly, being able to understand what is shown to him in a book, or following instructions. Sometimes a parent can be infuriated that a child just isn't "getting it"—yet it may not be the child's fault. Sometimes children literally don't hear or see what we hear or see. Listen to this boy describing his sensory problems:

"A trick that my ears played was to change the volume of sounds around me. Sometimes when other kids spoke to me I could scarcely hear them, and sometimes they sounded like bullets. I thought I was going to go deaf."
(Darren, age twelve)

2. **Organization** This involves adding new information to what you already have, and also sequencing information. For instance, you might see the number 231 but store it as 213.

3. **Memory** Everyone knows about this one! When you go to get it out again, it's still there! There are both short-term and long-term memory abilities—and sometimes one is impaired and not the other.

4. **Output** Can you make sense as you speak, write, or draw? The knowledge is in there—can you get it out?

Clearly it's good to get professional help if you suspect your child is having trouble. Many learning difficulties can be overcome or at least minimized. The earlier you act, the easier this will be.

OCCUPATIONAL THERAPY

Here is an instance of a boy overcoming an output problem—handwriting.

David, age eight, had a lot of trouble with handwriting. Poor handwriting isn't unusual for boys at this age, but David's parents were worried because he hadn't improved at all for two years. They knew that David was a bright child, but they feared that because of his poor written work teachers might think he was dumb.

STORIES FROM THE HEART

A Middle School Doing a Great Job with Boys

Staff at Ashfield Boys High School in Sydney, Australia, wanted to make learning more personal, believing that the closer the relationship between the teacher and the student, the more effective the learning would be.

"We were trying to analyze what was wrong. The boys were not as engaged with learning and were not as successful as they should be," Ashfield principal Ann King told Jane Figgis in the *Sydney Morning Herald*.

So Ashfield restructured its seventh- and eighth-grade classes in a dramatic way. "Instead of having ten to thirteen teachers, boys now have a team of five teachers, who not only teach but are responsible for discipline, welfare, and parent liaison."

Sessions have been extended from the usual forty minutes to eighty or one hundred minutes, after it was realized students were having small parcels of learning that were not connected and teachers who were not connected.

"We have found it works tremendously well," Ms. King says. "On many measures we are seeing that they are more actively and successfully engaged in their learning. The real value, however, of teaching teams and students who stay together as a group through the school day, and year, is the potential for the students and their teachers to develop much more solid and collaborative relationships."

Relationships are the key in middle school. "Students and teachers have to learn to listen to each other, to trust each other, to like each other. They need to be able to challenge each other, but that can only happen when they feel at ease and secure in the relationship," said Ms. King.

A Primary School Doing a Great Job with Boys

Darley School, in western Victoria, Australia, is a bright light in its rural community. Many of the kids have challenges in their lives, but the school is responding to this. It is a visually bright and appealing place, from the front gate murals to the walls that seem to feature every child in photos and awards and activities. Sixth-grade teacher Melanie Hughes told me about their Lizard Lounge, an innovation that was beyond anything I had seen before. The school had realized that a boys' class was just the thing for the sixth-grade year, when girls were bounding ahead in body and mind and boys were turning off from learning and finding it hard to keep up. A boys' sixth grade was introduced—an innovation that I am seeing, especially in the final year of primary school, as having great benefits. Melanie and her principal, Anne Summall, felt the boys needed not just their own class, but also a curriculum focus that would engage their practical minds and draw out their nurturing qualities.

A reptile collection was the answer. Each boy studied to qualify as a reptile caregiver and took on care of a lizard, snake, or other creature. Today, other schools come to visit Darley to see the lizards and admire the way the boys take care of them, and to learn academic skills and motivation at the same time.

The normal way to improve handwriting is through lots of practice—practicing big swirls and shapes, getting smaller, learning individual letters, gradually building up the skills of easy writing. But David's parents spoke to someone who suggested they try something else as well—occupational therapy.

Kerry Anne Brown, an occupational therapist experienced in children's learning difficulties, agreed to see David for an evaluation. Kerry Anne discovered that David was poorly coordinated in his whole upper body, not just in his hands. In fact, it was hard for him to write well because he did not sit well or hold his arms in a strong, firm way.

Was this inherited, or caused by damage at birth or (later) lack of exercise? Who knows? An occupational therapist's job is to get the body working as best it can, whatever the cause.

David began doing exercises (balance, spinning, trampolining) to strengthen his back muscles and build up coordination of his back, shoulders, and arms. This required a six-month program of about half an hour a day. Luckily, the exercises were a lot of fun, and his dad and mom really enjoyed the exercise time with him. Sometimes the harder parts made David grumpy, but overcoming frustration is part of any new learning. His parents cajoled and humored him and kept him going. After about six months, the program was getting good results and they were able to stop.

Three years later, David still has to "make himself" write well—which means relaxing his body and really paying attention. But his writing is now good for a boy his age. Although he would rather use a computer to write, he enjoys creative writing and was recently the valedictorian of his primary school.

PARENTS MAKE IT HAPPEN

Learning difficulties require two things—time and resources—and these have to be fought for. Kids whose parents care about them and are willing to spend time with them will always fare better. It takes determination—tracking down specialist help, refusing to be ignored, and pushing the school system to get special help. Be sure to talk to other parents and be proactive until something happens that works for your child.

Resources include special programs or equipment, specialist teachers, classes, and things you can do at home. Meeting other parents whose children have the same problem as your child can be a huge help. It's great to get information and emotional support from people who really understand.

A note of caution: occasionally you may encounter schools that do not want to know about learning-disabled kids. They are more interested in the elite achievers who keep up the school's academic average. A school might not help a learning-disabled child, or it could actually pressure the child to leave. Caring schools will always do their best, and you wouldn't want your child in a school that did not care for all its kids, anyway.

In a Nutshell

Schools can be good places for boys if they do the following.

1. Allow boys to start school one year later than girls, when their fine-motor skills are ready for pencil-and-paper work. (Girls' skills develop more quickly.)

2. Vigorously recruit males (young and mature age) into teaching and also involve more of the right kind of men from the community to provide one-on-one coaching and support.

3. Redesign schooling to be more physical, energetic, concrete, and challenging.

4. Target boys' weak areas (literacy especially) with boy-specific intensive language programs, right from first grade (and have separate English classes in junior high and high school).

5. Build good personal relationships with boys, through smaller classes and fewer teacher changes in high school, so as to meet boys' needs for fathering and mentoring.

6. Be alert to the fact that problem behavior can be a sign of learning difficulties and investigate this as soon as possible.

Boys and Sports

Every Christmas our extended family (five sisters, their husbands and children and grandparents, and one or two extras) gathers together from far and wide at one of the family's places in Tasmania. We oldsters watch with delight as the youngsters are instantly at ease again, as if the intervening year since last Christmas simply hadn't happened.

We eat Poppy's vegetables and Nana's cooking, then settle down to a game of cricket in the field out back. I've watched this for twenty years now, since the children could barely hold onto a bat. What is most amazing in these once-a-year games is the way that the men, normally quiet guys on the whole, seem to come out of themselves on the playing field. It's a very child-oriented game, and no one keeps score. A little boy attempts to bat; the men praise and encourage him, visibly leaning closer as if to will him to success. An eight-year-old struggles with overhand bowling, sends the ball wildly off course, and old men call out "Good one!" and "That's better!" Small hints are whispered. Somebody rushes in to correct a grip. A kid gets out for a duck and is allowed to stay in so he can have a hit.

It's not all peace and light. Two of the ten-year-old boys are at the stage of being obsessed with rules. There is a dispute; a boy yells abuse. His father takes him off to the side for a quiet talking-to. The gist of it is, "Feelings are important here. It's only a game"—a hard thing for a ten-year-old to digest. Sports are a lot about character building.

Play goes on. Under the hot sun I am transported back in time, wondering how the older men learned these ways of being with children—a tradition of caring for the young that goes back to the very roots of human history. Sports can be an unbeatable medium for caring, learning, and bringing the generations together.

Sports: A Double-Edged Sword

For most boys, sports are a huge part of life. It can do them a lot of good. It can give them a sense of belonging, develop character, boost self-esteem and good health. But it can also do a lot of harm: it can cripple them in body, warp them in mind, teach them bad values, and lead to a crushing sense of failure.

All through our history human beings have played sports. Even in the dark age, people played early forms of football. Almost all cultures had running races. The Romans had gladiators and the Greeks had the Olympics. And although not solely a male preserve, sports have appealed to boys in particular—perhaps as an outlet for their explosive energies and a chance to excel at something that doesn't require talking or neatness!

Sports mean respect—in most industrial nations today, sports are virtually a sacred activity. No religion comes close in its passion, the sheer number of its adherents, or its power to inspire. So, for virtually every parent of boys, dealing with sports is a major interest and challenge.

The Positives of Sports

Sports offer a boy a chance to get closer to his father, and to other boys and men, through a common interest they might otherwise lack. Complete strangers can discuss it—including fathers and sons! Many men will tell you, "If my old man and I couldn't talk about sports, we would have nothing to talk about at all."

A SAFE PLACE TO SHOW AFFECTION

A friend of mine was once persuaded to join a men's indoor cricket team. He wasn't keen. To use his own words, he expected to be "bored stupid by macho rubbish." But he was amazed to find it was nothing like that. The men were incredibly affectionate toward each other. There was real praise for effort, exchange of hints and skills, warmth, and (through good-natured teasing) much affirmation of the younger men's energy and skill, and the older men's experience and perspective. And in the after-game sessions, real concerns and life challenges were discussed. The thing that struck my friend was that he knew some of these men in their families and in the business world, *and they were nothing like this anywhere else.* Somehow the structure and rituals of the team allowed each man to be a fuller, happier self. My friend enjoyed the experience immensely.

Because sports offer the main place where men and boys interact, it is often where boys can work through, in a practical way, their values for life. From a tender age, when they can barely hold a bat or ball, little boys begin to learn how to:

- Be a good loser (and not cry, punch someone, or run away if you lose)
- Be a good winner (to be modest and so avoid making others feel bad)
- Be part of a team (to play cooperatively, recognize your limitations, and support others' efforts)
- Give it your best effort (to train even when you are tired and continue to try your hardest)
- Work for a long-term goal or objective (and make sacrifices to achieve it)
- See that almost everything you do in life improves with practice

Parents will go to endless trouble so that their kids can play sports. The benefits are clear—fun, fitness, and fresh air, character building, friendship, and a sense of achievement and belonging. And the kids get a lot out of it, too!

The Negatives

On the darker side, sports are changing, and not always for the better. There are hazards to body and mind, and parents have to steer a little more carefully than a generation ago. Let's explore why.

TOXIC ROLE MODELS AND THE "JOCK" CULTURE

Sports and sporting heroes are an obsession for our whole society. Imagine if someone suggested that we devote the last ten minutes of the evening news to woodworking or stamp collecting! Sports set fashion, command huge incomes, carry the hope of national pride. Sports figures are instantly recognized, while great musicians, artists, writers (of parenting books . . .) are barely noticed.

We parents want to use the power of sports to make our kids better people. But it can just as easily work the other way. Especially in male sports, impressionable children receive all kinds of unwholesome messages from men who never really grew up.

Where are you most likely to see real-life demonstrations of violence, egotism, bad temper, sexual crudity, alcohol abuse, racism, and homophobia? At any sports field! A boy may learn to be courageous and strong by playing baseball or football, but he may also learn to binge drink, use drugs, and mistreat women.

STORIES FROM THE HEART

The Coach from Hell!

Fourteen-year-old Marcus loved to play rugby. Because his school didn't field a team for his age group, his dad, Jeff, took him to a local club that had a team. This team had made it to the finals three years in a row but never won that final game.

To overcome this, a special coach was hired—an aggressive ex-footballer—to train the forwards. Jeff watched from the sidelines as the new coach spoke to the boys. He was shocked to hear his instructions. "As soon as you encounter the other team's players, hit them hard in the face."

One of the boys wasn't sure if he'd heard right. "Is that, uh, if they hit you, do you mean?" he stammered.

"No, you idiot! You punch them before they get the chance. Understand?"

Jeff felt himself shaking with anger. This was not his idea of what the sport was about. That night, he phoned a friend who also coached rugby. He confirmed that punching was against the rules and could lead to a suspension—and was just plain wrong!

Jeff realized he had to confront the coach. The coach dismissed him laughingly: "Huh, those wimps, they wouldn't do it anyway! I'm just trying to give them some steel, the little pansies."

So, is this a coach who doesn't expect his advice to be taken, or is showing a slippery double standard? Either way, Jeff decided this wasn't any place for a boy to learn. Father and son talked it over, and Marcus was happy to quit the team. The following year, he played at his school, on a team that was coached by a better kind of man.

"Looking back," Jeff told me later, "I'd known all along that the team had no spirit—the coaches constantly put the boys down, there was no group feeling, no praise, no enjoyment. And despite making it to three grand finals, they were always made to feel like failures."

Marcus was a whole lot happier on his new team, and his dad was pleased to have recognized the problem and found a better alternative.

Doping, cheating, using steroids, the added tensions and pressures that arise from sponsorship, and the huge salaries paid to successful sports figures all act to damage and distort the purity of sports and its happy and healthy role for children. And too often the adults of the game introduce these elements.

Sports leaders—coaches, trainers, parents, and officials—are like elders of the tribe. They should remember that sports are games, and that sports are for the players, not players for the sports (or the sponsor). If sports don't better equip our youngsters for real life, we are better off going fishing.

THE TALENT TRAP

Success can be a much bigger problem than failure. Few boys today get adequate male attention. If a boy shows promise in football, baseball, soccer, or tennis, adults suddenly take an interest in him. His father or coach showers him with praise. His name and photo are in the local paper; strangers praise him in the street. The men get a vehicle for their own frustrated dreams; the boy gets the approval he craves.

Being a sports hero gives a boy an artificial sense of his own importance. His access to adoring girls and even adult "sucking up" will set him up for an inevitable collision with reality.

But what if the boy injures himself? What if he reaches his natural limitations? What if he resorts to performance drugs to keep up with expectations, or he overtrains and becomes exhausted? The approval falls away, the older men show their disappointment. Community praise turns to rejection. Thousands of young lives have been harmed in this way. The more talented a child is, the more important it is that parents guard against "sports abuse"—not letting an adult agenda disrupt the normal tasks of adolescence.

How Role-Modeling Works

The nature of youngsters is to take in their role models and swallow them whole. If a man is a good basketball player, then boys will want to imitate not just his ball skills, but also his attitudes and his lifestyle. (This is the basis of all sponsorship and the massive global industry around merchandising and sports.)

If schools want to persuade teenagers not to smoke, to practice safer sex, or to pick up litter, they bring in a sports star. If a business wants to inspire their sales reps to sell more accounting software (for instance), they get in a Hall of Famer! It borders

on the bizarre, but it shows how much sports have become the measure of maleness.

Luckily, as we mature as a society, we find there are more diverse ways to be a man. A boy may admire and learn from a musician, an artist, a craftsman, a dancer, a filmmaker, or a fly fisherman. This means that there is more range of possibility for every kind of boy to find his true path. Perhaps one day soon we will have so many good men in the lives of children that they will be able to develop a widely based, rich, and really life-inspiring identity. "That man is like me, and I can be like that man" will be true for every boy.

What about Injuries?

Sports are healthy, aren't they? Not always. Men's health researcher Richard Fletcher found that for some sports it was healthier to stay home and watch TV! Many top athletes and sportsmen have painful and crippling injuries by the time they are thirty. These range from head injuries to countless damaged joints and tendons. Sporting sprains and pains often lead to painful arthritis in midlife. It's becoming clear that certain sports are no longer a good risk for kids.

In the United States, each year tens of thousands of children are seen in accident and emergency departments as a result of sports injuries. (And this figure doesn't include those taken to medical centers, physiotherapists, and so on.) About two thousand of these injuries can be classed as serious, involving long-term treatment or hospitalization. Body-contact sports cause the highest number of injuries. Football has almost double the injury rates of soccer and basketball, all more dangerous than noncontact sports such as baseball and tennis. But a lot lies in the way a sport is played and managed. Overtraining is still the greatest injury category, suggesting some coaches overwork their players.

Injuries sustained by school children playing sports include sprains, strained muscles, bruising, and broken bones. There have been a number of deaths of boys playing rugby in recent years, as well as a worrying number of head injuries and spinal injuries. And the risk of sports injuries increases with age. On average, between the ages of twelve and sixteen, the injury rate increases *sevenfold*. (Testosterone at work!)

The real problem is competition. Being overly competitive leads to risk-taking, aggression, and going beyond sensible physical limits. *Adults are to blame for this.* Children by and large prefer to have fun; they are not fanatical unless we make them so.

We're not suggesting you keep your boys away from sport. The need to test oneself in physical ways, to experience moderate levels of competition—for the fun of it—and the sheer benefits of spending lots of time being active and in the open air, means that sports are always going to be a winner for boys' health and development. We just have to choose the sport carefully and be involved in seeing that it's well run and devoted to the kids, not the other way around.

Make It Good

Right this minute, all around the globe, groups of children are laughing and shouting with joy, as they play sports and games. And adults and children are spending time together, experiencing the joy of encouragement and effort, of having something in common, and of knowing that life is about more than work and worry. A basketball hoop in the backyard or a nearby park where others gather companionably for a pickup game is a happy place to be.

For the most part, sports are a beautiful part of life. If adults understand sports, enjoy them with their kids, guide their kids into the right attitudes, and remember what sports are really for, then all will be well.

In a Nutshell

1. Sports can have huge benefits for children. Sports offer exercise, fun, challenges, and a sense of achievement. Sports especially provide a shared interest between fathers and sons, and boys and men generally.

2. Sports are often a great way of building character, learning about life, and developing masculinity.

3. Unfortunately, sports are changing for the worse. The culture of some sports encourages negative traits like aggression, egotism, sexual crudity, and binge drinking. And "winning at all costs" is replacing sportsmanship and the pleasure of playing the game for its own sake.

4. When competition and winning are made so important, it is dangerous to be talented, because your life becomes unbalanced. Playing sports too competitively often leads to lifelong injuries.

5. Emphasizing competition excludes many kids who are not so talented. Research is finding that more and more boys have stopped playing sports.

6. Sports must be participatory, safe, nonelitist, and fun for everyone. Boys need sports. We must not let commercial forces or toxic leadership spoil them.

CHAPTER TEN

A Community Challenge

The spirit of a boy is too great for just a family to contain, and his horizons are wider than a family can provide for. By his mid-teens, a boy wants to leap into his future—but there must be a place for him to leap to, and strong arms to steady him. This means building community links in order to help boys.

If we parents have community around us, then we can trust that other adults, singly or as an organized group, can support our teenagers into a sense of worth and belonging. Without community—networks of committed adults consciously caring for each other's children—adolescence can actually fail as a life stage.

The transition into adulthood takes concerted effort. But how is it done? What are the methods and what is the timetable? What are the key elements? Some are practical: a listening ear, the teaching of skills, the expansion into new horizons of thinking and action, the giving of cautions and protection from danger. Some are more "magical" and spiritual.

To illustrate, and to give a fitting ending to this book, I have chosen three stories. Each is a story about community action turning boys into men. Each story is very different—a football match, a school on the poor side of town, and an island sojourn. Read on.

Losing, Winning, and Grace

The annual match between Sydney's two proud Catholic schools, St. Joseph's College and Riverview, has always assumed epic proportions in the minds of those who follow rugby union.

St. Joseph's record against all schools is somewhat awesome. It's the kind of record that gave mystical impossibility to the idea of wresting it from them!

The year 1996, however, was different. Riverview knew they had a great team capable of achieving the impossible. So on this day, under a clear blue sky, there was a special sense of history. As the game progressed, it became evident to the fifteen thousand or so parents and alumni who gathered to watch that the unthinkable was going to happen—St. Joseph's was going to lose that day. Despite valiant attempts by the St. Joseph's boys in the last half, clawing their way back up the score table, the Riverview team held the lead. Soon the final siren signaled an end to St. Joseph's long reign.

The match was over—the victors punched the air and whooped around. Then something powerful and special began to take place. The losing team formed into a ring on the oval, linked arms, and stood as if in prayer—absorbing not so much the loss as something more; perhaps the sense of shared effort, the sheer poignancy of the moment. Then the real magic began. Like an answer from around the stadium, men who had gone to that school, and fathers of the boys, walked toward the circle and wrapped their arms around the ring of boys. Several hundred men ended up in a silent, powerful ring of masculine grace.

People pouring from the stands froze in place and just watched. Losing or winning lost all meaning at the sight of this. It was the sense of union through effort, of giving yourself to something larger—as ancient as the mammoth hunt, the defense of the city, or the thousand other ways men have stood together for *good* reasons. And it was the honoring and welcoming of youth into its glory.

No one who was in that circle will forget it. Each became more of a man because of that day.

Men at Work

A large company in New Zealand was wanting to do something for its local community—nothing altruistic about this, just good business sense. The usual thing might be to endow a youth center or build a park. Some wise souls persuaded them to "adopt" a local school in the run-down neighborhood where their plant was situated—and to contribute not dollars but time.

Every employee was given the opportunity to go to the school and offer one-on-one coaching to a child who needed help with math, reading, or motor skills. They could do this for two hours a week on work time. The school coordinated the program; the company donated the manpower and womanpower.

The result was that at-risk children got two visits a week in school time from their own long-term special adult. The effect of the program was so significant that over two years, the school's national testing scores improved markedly. And that was only one outcome—think of the self-esteem, the mentoring, and the long-term outcomes in turning kids toward positive lifestyles.

What would happen if we took the do-gooder energies of our service clubs and corporations (and so on) and built *human contact* instead of, or as well as, checkbook approaches to making kids' lives a little richer? It's hard to know where such an involvement would stop. Getting to know kids in trouble changes your perspective. Benefits flow both ways. Perhaps it would work in an organization you belong to? This kind of thing *could* change the world.

Initiation

It's autumn on an island off Australia's beautiful coastline. Three days earlier, twelve men with backpacks and coats, and nine teenage boys ranging from fourteen to nineteen, jostled onto the ferry to cross to the island. Now they are awaiting its return to carry them home. Their mood is reflective and serene, like the glassy water around the sheltered landing place.

Seven of the boys are sons of the men; two are boys without fathers. Some of the men are married; a couple are separated. One is a single father.

Once they arrived on the island, they walked to a remote shack where they cooked lunch, explored, played, and swam at a wild and windswept beach. At night, they carried coats and walked through the darkness to a place where a fire had been prepared beforehand, and sat down—the boys nervous and joking, wondering what was to happen.

Around the fire, each of the twelve men stood up and spoke about his own life. Some spoke with humor, some were faltering and emotional. After this, each father stood again and spoke on behalf of his own son. He spoke about the qualities of his son, his own special memories, and how much he loved this boy. The boys without fathers received this praise equally from one of the men who was there to represent them—adding messages sent from a grandfather and a father in prison.

Fathers openly praising their sons! There was something so unique in this experience that many of the men and boys were wet-eyed in the half-light of the flames. Somehow these tears were soothing and sweet—the very opposite of grief or shame.

After the men finished, each boy then spoke for himself in reply (with surprising eloquence) about his life, his values, and hopes.

Later that weekend, the boys and men split into small groups, talking about the boys' plans for their lives and their goals for the coming year. These goals were announced ritually in a final meeting of the whole group. One boy said he wanted to go back to school and finish his senior year, another wanted to get a job, another to stop depending on drugs, several to right wrongs they had committed, one to find a girlfriend, and another to "make it work out with Mom."

Adults offered support to each young man: one offered somewhere to study; another a meeting for coffee once a month to follow up. One man committed to drive a boy to Adelaide to make amends to a grandmother he had stolen money from. The group agreed to meet one year later to reaffirm their care for the youngsters.

Since my book *Manhood* was published, hundreds of people have asked me for information about initiating youngsters into adulthood. Some cultures—Jewish, Islamic, and others— have preserved initiatory and sacred processes for moving boys into manhood. The aboriginal traditions and stories are not all lost and may be of great value. Although some aspects of our society are in a time of disintegration, all around us are the bits and pieces of wisdom of the many cultures that we come from. We simply have to make our own ways. What will matter most to our boys is that we make the effort.

STORIES FROM THE HEART

How Having a Son Has Changed Me

by Sarah MacDonald

Sarah MacDonald is an Australian writer, journalist and radio broadcaster who for a long time didn't understand males. Having a son changed everything. As she began to love him, it began to heal her, too. A beautiful story to end the book.

I'm as much of a fan of martial arts as I am of major dental work. But this week, as I watched my little boy wrap a white belt around his skinny waist, join a line of his mates and learn to kick, my heart swelled with love. Having a son has changed so much about how I view the world. From understanding martial arts, to healing a fraught sibling relationship and possibly, in some ways, even how I think about men.

I have two brothers, but the brother closest in age to me was a "frenemy." We would play beautifully for snatches, but as we got older we increasingly fought—violently, loudly and mercilessly. I was constantly annoyed by his exuberance, his ever-ready energy and what I saw as his aggression. I then went off to an all-girls high school and boys become a mystery until they became an obsession. Since then, my male mates and my husband have taught me a terrific amount about being a bloke, but seeing a son grow up is giving me a cellular, visceral and emotional understanding.

My son looks a lot like the brother I battled. He even talks, walks and acts in a manner that transports me back to being nine years old. I can see myself in his older sister as she slams the bedroom door in his pleading face. I feel his hurt at the rejection so deeply I wish I could rewind time to apologize to his uncle. I now understand what happens on the other side of that door; the sweetness and vulnerability of the boy that battles.

While my daughter lives in an imaginary world of her own creation, my son is firmly grounded on earth. I can see his body constantly craving excitement, sensation and physicality; hence the tackling, hugging, hitting and whacking of friends and his family. While I used to be furious at my brother for picking up and wielding every stick he saw and destroying every single toy we had—I see my son as a physical entity making sense of the world with his body. I feel my daughter's pain at the consequences but realize she usually gives as good as she gets. Perhaps I've edited my own violence out of my story.

My son's need for physical sensations even wake him most nights. He still comes into our bedroom, so I wake nearly daily to the brush of his soft warm cheek and puffs of tiny breath inches from my face.

His nonverbal communication is another understanding he's given me about boys. While he's often a chatty young thing, my son doesn't need to talk about everything. In fact, when he's most emotional, the verbal part of his brain shuts down. His first sentence at age three was "Mom, just stop talking!" Sometimes, less really is more.

While my daughter can fool me rather easily, my son is more transparent when he's been naughty. His body betrays him; a tight twist to his mouth, his long-lashed eyes cast to the side and shoulders hunched. When I ask, "What have you done?" he'll reply, "Nothing, but don't look under my bed." When I then find the party animal or diary he's stolen from his sister, he's astonished by his inability at subterfuge.

There's also purity in his passion. My son loves music. As do all his friends. They dance rapturously; connecting with a primal, deep, beautiful and spiritual rhythm. I pray the day never comes when they get self-conscious and resort to the goofy white-boy shuffle. The girls sing to hairbrushes and do their jazz ballet but for the boys, the music is glue that binds them to one another and to their bodies. They absorb it totally, recklessly and powerfully. They meet in its beats as their bodies meet in space.

I see my son's friendships, forged on the dance floor and the martial arts hall, in all their glory. I am coming to understand the visceral need boys have to belong. I've always bristled at the word "gang" but now feel my son's desire to bond; his band of brothers feel confident and secure in their unity and they love each other deeply.

I once heard a male educator say humor is a great way to connect with boys. He's right. My son may not need to talk but he frequently needs to laugh. He has a fabulous sense of the ridiculousness in life and doesn't always try to make sense of it. I can see the male sense of humor forming and I honor it as much as his tears of pain. Perhaps this generation of young men, far less likely to be told, "Stop crying, boys don't cry," will keep showing that vulnerability.

While hearing my son's glorious giggle and watching him negotiate the rigors of school and a world of complications, I ache for his vulnerable spirit. I can now see my brother's softness, bruised heart and good nature. And at times, I find it easier to see the boy in other men. As a bonus, my brother has had a little girl. It's beautiful to watch him begin a journey of understanding from the other side.

Appendix A

Practical Notes on ADHD in Boys

ADHD (Attention Deficit Hyperactivity Disorder) is a diagnostic label for a cluster of problem behaviors that have become alarmingly common in the past twenty years, especially in boys. This cluster usually includes distractibility, forgetfulness, poor impulse control, and hyperactivity—moving about all the time. It's not hard to spot. Please note that ADD (Attention Deficit Disorder) involves different symptoms and treatments from ADHD.

Approximately 5 percent of boys in the United States, and somewhat less in various other countries, are both given this diagnosis and treated with fairly significant amphetamine medication.

That such an epidemic might occur—without precedent and without any known mechanism or physical cause—has shocked and concerned many people. Is it our culture of rush and hurry that prevents little children from learning to be calm and focused? Is it the way schools unreasonably expect little boys to sit still? Is it too much TV preventing the skills of attention from developing? Is it stress at home and parents not meeting children's needs early in life? Is it greedy drug companies wanting to hook everyone on their products? Is it something different in the brain? Is it passed on in a family's genes?

The answer—and this is not a cop-out—is probably a combination of all of these things.

Prominent Canadian psychiatrist Gabor Mate has done more than any other researcher in recent years to help progress our thinking on ADHD. Gabor was a Holocaust baby, born just before the Nazi invasion of Hungary, and he has ADHD. So do his three children.

In his book *Scattered: How Attention Deficit Disorder Originates, and What You Can Do About It,* Gabor talks vividly about the experience of having ADHD from the inside. He is convinced from his own experience and from that of his clients that ADHD is a *developmental delay.* Parts of the brain do not grow in the second six months of life, because caregivers or parents are too stressed or distracted to pass on calm and soothing attention, which normally triggers the growth of attending and calming areas of the cortex. These areas are found to be unusually thin and undeveloped in brain scans of people with ADHD. Only some children get ADHD because only some inherit the vulnerability. You need both the genetics and the environment to get ADHD. The best part of this understanding is that if ADHD is a delay, then brain growth can be stimulated by new learning and help later on.

Gabor's main message is love, patience, and time. He believes in helping children by teaching them strategies to calm themselves and focus. Professional help from psychologists specializing in this is often essential, and most experts recommend that medication on its own is never enough. Medication carries risks and should be used only if needed, and in order to gain a window of time to help and teach the child. Generally, the effects of medication weaken over time, so it's essential that families are given more help than just a prescription.

ADHD is real. But it also can be mistakenly diagnosed, and it's important to look at all possible causes of the troublesome behavior—what might be stressing the child in the home, school, or other locations. All these have to be investigated before the label is applied, because many things in life result in kids like this: abuse, family discord, trauma, grief, and so on.

A final note: many adults also have ADHD. I have most of the symptoms, and had some tough times as a child and teenager as a result. So I certainly recommend love and understanding and patience.

Along with Gabor Mate's book, some recommended ADHD parenting books are listed in the Notes section.

Appendix B

How to Tell Whether a School Is a Good One for Boys

Say you wanted to choose a school for your son. How would you know whether it was a good one? Apart from the obvious—happy, courteous, and cheerful kids on the school grounds, and happy, courteous, and cheerful staff in the building—there are some things to look for and questions to ask.

You might not want to use all of these, but they are a good guide. And, for a school evaluating itself, they are vital.

1. **It knows how it is doing with boys, and can tell you.** The school keeps track of how individual boys, and boys as a whole, are doing on a range of criteria, including engagement in school activities and school life, academic effort, progress and results, behavior and relationships, sporting and social life, and leadership.
   Key question: What statistics does the school publish about boys' progress?

2. **It has policies and practices based on a positive approach to maleness.** The school knows what it values in boys and men, based on asking parents, teachers, and girls and boys themselves, and it celebrates and honors this positive view of what boys can be.

Key question: Does the school have a mission statement about which qualities it likes, wants, and values in boys?

3. **It uses teaching and assessment styles that appeal to boys' strengths.** This means recognizing the likely maturational, physical, and social differences between boys and girls, and having positive approaches to these—such as late starting for boys, physical and activity-based teaching and assessment methods in all grades and all subjects, and catering for kinesthetic, visual, and musical intelligence as well as linguistic and logical.
   Key question: How does the school accommodate the specific developmental, physical, social, and learning needs of boys in its teaching and assessment?

4. **It has behavior policies and procedures that help boys gain a positive identity and a positive relationship with others.** This means that discipline or behavior procedures are based on agreed-upon values, with the aim of having fair, equitable, and fun relationships among everyone in the school. Male and female staff should be good models of this type of relationship.
   Key question: Do teachers shout at children at this school?

5. **It has school structures that are likely to suit boys.** This means having a flexible approach to scheduling, which can allow for: single-sex classes for some subjects at certain ages (for example, third grade and middle-school years); school to work programs; longer class periods in the morning; fewer changes of teacher; and two-year blocks with the same teacher.

Key question: How does the timetable allow for boys' special need for more settled and sometimes separate learning?

6. **It ensures that boys have access to a range of male mentors and role models.** This means recognizing that male staff and volunteers have a special role in relation to boys. It also requires tackling the question of what qualities the school seeks in its male staff (apart from just being male).
   Key question: What personality criteria are used to select male staff at this school?

7. **It is democratic.** This means that for all students, including boys, there should be genuine participation in deciding how the school is run—in the real issues of classroom learning and what the school offers.
   Key question: How are boys involved in decision making here?

8. **It offers many different ways to gain recognition.** Not all boys are good at math or at football. There must be ways in which all boys can gain recognition. Highly competitive regimes with prizes for the top few do not suit boys.
   Key question: How do shy, overweight, arty, or simply average boys achieve recognition at this school?

9. **It involves fathers and father figures from the community.** In most schools, the ratio of female to male volunteers is about six to one. It is a myth that dads are too busy, or don't care, or aren't good at school activities.

But they will not get involved without some real creative effort from the school.

Key question: What is your strategy for getting dads and other community men involved?

10. **It is continually active in learning how to do better with boys.** Male and female teachers can learn from each other about what works and why. Because new issues about boys' education are coming to light, there should be ongoing in-service training, research, and evaluation regarding effective education for boys.

    Key question: Do you have ongoing staff development and research into what works best for boys within the school?

This list was devised by Deborah Hartman and Richard Fletcher, Boys to Fine Men Program, University of Newcastle, New South Wales.

Acknowledgments

When I was little, my mother would always talk to me and explain things, and we would go on long walks around the town (I was in the stroller!). Today I make my living with words, and love the wind in my hair. So, thanks Mum.

Dad was good at playing with us—tickling and wrestling. We had a good start in the wet green hills and windy beaches of North Yorkshire.

Australia has been kind to me—friends at school, teachers who cared, and employers who gave me a chance to try out new things. While (like most young men) I have known a lot of pain and confusion, there was always someone who showed kindness and turned things around.

I was blessed beyond belief to meet Shaaron. I'd have been a much lesser parent, therapist, and human being without her. Thank you, Shaaron—especially for our children. As young adults now, my kids have also contributed greatly to making me a better person, and assisted to carry out my work. My Uniting Church community has been supportive and helpful in making me a braver activist, especially in working to end Australia's maltreatment of refugee boat people. We succeeded, eventually, in ending a horrible regime and bringing about change. Australia is now a kinder and more just country.

Judi Taylor has organized my seminars in Sydney as a personal mission, and together we have reached tens of thousands of people. Judi and her husband, Paul, gave great help, input, and encouragement with this book. Paul told me the story of the historic school football match in the final chapter.

The Playgroups Association in Australia, TREATS in Hong Kong, Doro Marden and Parent Network in England, and hundreds of community groups and school districts have sponsored wonderful tours and seminars. Ian Ochiltree organized national theater speaking tours across the UK. Waldorf Schools in the United States helped me learn about the American childhood experience.

Rex Finch, a warm, principled, and dynamic publisher and a longtime friend, was able to work with me in creative ways that improved the results beyond the capabilities of either one of us. Peter Vogel, Peter Whitcombe, Paul Whyte, and Dr. Rex Stoessiger all shared their expertise generously. Sean Doyle taught me a lot about writing well. Sara Golski and Kristi Hein did a phenomenal job of helping me create this U.S. edition for Ten Speed Press/Celestial Arts.

We love Paul Stanish's cartoons and Steve Miller's beautiful design. Dr. Jenny Harasty was generous with her time and ideas on helping boys communicate. Alison Soutter sent great material on gender identity disorder.

Though the opinions about ADHD in this book are completely my own responsibility, pediatrician Dr. David McDonald helped enormously with research material and advice about finding a middle road on ADHD.

Lyn and John Sykes read the manuscript and contributed stories. So did many other people who will recognize themselves but can't be identified. Thank you so much.

Notes

Chapter 1

Page 2 " . . . boys don't read books any more": West, Peter, "Giving Boys a Ray of Hope; Masculinity and Education." Discussion paper for Gender Equity Taskforce, Australia, February 1995.

Page 3 "They pretend not to care about anything . . .": Hudson, M., & Carr, L., "Ending Alienation," in *The Gen*, Department of Education and Training newsletter on gender equity in schools, June 1966. These researchers reported that "perhaps surprisingly, it's the very boys who are always in trouble and appear not to care who most want to succeed. . . . [teachers] were staggered to find that those students *did* want to do well at school and saw school achievement as important. One high school took a look at the students who were sent to the 'time out' room and found they were nearly all boys, and they all had literacy problems. We found that kids *want to be successful in school*—even the ones who give the impression they don't care. And that message was repeated over and over [in the findings]."

Page 3 Boys acting "aggressive and unpleasant": This is not "a stage they are going through." Several long-term studies have found it disturbingly easy to predict criminality and drug and drunk-driving behavior by assessing boys as young as six. For instance: "The way boys act at six years of age is a reliable predictor of whether they will turn into teenage drug and alcohol abusers', say researchers in the United States and Canada. Louise Musse of the University of Texas in Houston and Richard Tremblay at the University of Montreal analyzed behavioral assessments of over a thousand boys who were followed from the age of six until they were sixteen. Musse and Tremblay report that boys who scored highly for hyperactiveness and fearlessness when aged six were likely to try drugs and get drunk in their early teens. These two measures successfully predict 75 percent of the boys who will later become drug and alcohol abusers, the researchers say. Musse and Tremblay argue that their findings could be used to target younger children in drug education programs." From *New Scientist*, 15 February 1997.

Page 3 "three times more likely than girls to die . . . from accidents, violence, and suicide . . .": Fletcher, Richard, *Australian Men and Boys: A Picture of Health?* Department of Health Studies, University of Newcastle, 1995. Richard Fletcher is the man most responsible for exposing Australia's dreadful record in men's and boys' health. He takes pains to point out that the problem is not a new one, but one that we have been conditioned to accept as normal. It is, nonetheless, an appalling waste of life and health.

Page 6 "Good News about Boys": "The Boys Are All Right," David von Drehle, *Time*, 6 August 2007; "America's Children, Key National Indicators of Well-Being," 2007, www.childstats.gov/americaschildren/.

Chapter 2

Page 13 " . . . she provides the milk . . .": Breastfeeding of babies provides them with nutrients that especially stimulate brain development. These nutrients are not currently present in formula milks. Children who are breastfed well into the first year of life are measurably more intelligent and also have greater immunity. In developing countries, breast milk is often the only safe means of infant feeding, yet bottle-feeding is often promoted aggressively by powdered-milk companies. This practice leads to over two million infant deaths each year, according to Community Aid Abroad.

Page 13 " . . . mothers like to calm them down": Phillips, Angela, *The Trouble with Boys*, Pandora, London, 1993.

Page 14 "Girl babies have a much better sense of touch": The "finger-touch sensitivity" in human females is many times greater than that of males. The difference is so great that there is no overlap between the genders—the least sensitive female is more sensitive than the most sensitive male.

Page 14 "Boys grow faster than girls and become stronger . . .": At birth boys are comparatively longer, heavier, and stronger (as measured by prone head reaction/grasp reflex). However, female infants are more mature at birth: girls' bones harden and their myelinization (development of the sheath surrounding the nerve fibers) proceeds more quickly in the first few years. Girls reach puberty sooner.

Normally, in adulthood a man will have a body-fat content of 15–18 percent. His female counterpart will have about 22–25 percent. His muscle will be more dense and his bones will be significantly stronger to support added weight and stress. On average, he will be 33 percent stronger.

Page 14 " . . . they are more troubled by separations . . .": Violato, C., & Russell, C., "Effects of Nonmaternal Care on Child Development," cited in Cook, Peter, *Early Childcare—Infants and Nations at Risk*, News Weekly Books, Melbourne, 1997. Also see Raphael, B., and Martinek, N., Department of Psychiatry, University of Queensland, "Men and Mental Health," report to Carmen Lawrence's First National Men's Health Conference, 1996.

Page 14 " . . . Boys in toddlerhood move around more and occupy more space": Phillips, Angela, *The Trouble with Boys*, Pandora, London, 1993. This is often seen in terms of boys "dominating" or "taking over" the space. In fact, this tendency to rush about and make a lot of noise is likely to be an anxiety response on the boys' part. This behavior is rarely observed in preschools that provide a very structured classroom environment and very concrete activities (such as Montessori schools), which boys enjoy.

Page 15 " . . . boys tend to ignore a new child who arrives in the group, whereas girls will notice them and befriend them . . .": Miedzian, Myriam, *Boys Will Be Boys—Breaking the Link Between Masculinity and Violence*, Virago, London, 1992.

Page 16 ". . . his brain may undergo physical changes to become a 'sad brain.'": University of Washington psychologist Geraldine Dawson found that depressed mothers raised babies with abnormally low levels of brain activity. If the mother rose above her depression to lavish care and energy on the baby, the baby recovered. Also, if the mother recovered before the baby was one year old, the baby completely recovered. If neither of these things happened, the child acquired a "sad brain" permanently. Reported in Nash, J. M., "Fertile Minds," *Time*, 3 February 1997.

Page 18 "boys are more prone than girls to separation anxiety and to becoming emotionally shut down . . .": Rafael and Martinek, "Men and Mental Health."

"There is much evidence to suggest that the mental health problems of male children are more extensive than female children and that these patterns will progressively change. Sex-related behavioural dispositions can be clearly identified and these may relate to temperament and to early socially reinforced behaviours, although there is substantial argument as to their biological components." p. 42

"Younger boys have a higher prevalence of mental health problems by approximately 2:1. Boys may be particularly sensitive to the influence of parental and family factors and their interaction with temperament." p. 43

"The boy will also be likely to be adversely affected by school environments which are negative." p. 43

Page 19 " . . . and make lots of noise": Gurian, Michael, *The Wonder of Boys*, Tarcher/Putnam, New York, 1996. Gurian's book gives a comprehensive look at boys' development, and he has become a leading figure in the U.S. media in speaking about boys' upbringing. He puts more weight than I would on the effects of testosterone, suggesting that it dominates a boy's psychology above all else. In doing this, the author tends to not leave a lot of room for individual variations or overlap between the genders. He advocates smacking boys (somehow not making the connection that this invariably makes them more violent). But these cautions aside, he has many good ideas and is worth reading.

Page 20 Silverstein, Olga, & Rashbaum, Beth, *The Courage to Raise Good Men*, Penguin, Melbourne, 1994. A good book, though rather narrowly focused on the one issue of mothers not pulling back from their children emotionally. Australian women do not tend to pull back from their children as sharply as American or British upper-class women do. Silverstein also seems to give little emphasis to the role of fathers.

Page 21 " . . . rather tense and brittle man": This kind of socialization of males is brilliantly depicted in several films, including *The Remains of the Day* starring Anthony Hopkins and *The Browning Version* with Albert Finney. Both are available on DVD and video.

Page 26 "Lighten up. Enjoy your kids . . .": "HSC robs young. There's more to life than exam results, Deane warns students" in the *Daily Telegraph*, 10 February 1997, p. 17. Australian Governor-General Sir William Deane told a parent group: "It is . . . essential that school students and parents keep a proper sense of proportion and pay due regard to the importance of community service, growing political awareness, cultural pursuits, social contacts and the sheer enjoyment of life."

Page 28 "A 1994 study of 180 boys and 78 girls": The study, headed by David Sandberg, a professor of pediatric psychiatry at the State University of New York at Buffalo, was published in the journal *Pediatrics*, cited in *San Francisco Chronicle*, 11, 1994, pp. 832–9.

Page 29 " . . . testosterone levels have increased by almost 800 percent!": At birth, a boy baby's testosterone levels are soaring at 250 mg/ml. From five to ten years of age, testosterone levels in the blood are as low as 30 mg/ml. At fifteen, they reach 600 mg/ml, which is the full adult level. From Semple, Michael, "How to Live Forever," *Esquire*, September 1993, page 127. See also Dow, S., "Hormone New Hope for Flagging Males" (*Age*, 19 May 1995, p. 11), which reports that testosterone affects the frequency of sexual behavior; Dabbs, J. M., "Testosterone, Crime and Misbehaviour Among Male Prison Inmates," *Journal of Personality and Individual Differences* (1995) 18:5, pp. 627–633, shows a strong link between testosterone levels and behavioral problems in prisons.

Page 33 Smith, Babette, *Mothers and Sons*, Allen & Unwin, Sydney, 1995, p. 20.

Page 42 **"What if he just can't hear?"**: Sax, Leonard, *Why Gender Matters*, Broadway Books, New York, 2005. Dr. Sax's endnotes detail many further studies and how they add up to this total picture. The following are just the most salient:

- Caine, Janel, "The Effects of Music on Selected Stress Behaviours, Weight, Caloric and Formula Intake and Length of Hospital Stay of Premature and Low Birthweight Neonates in a Newborn Intensive Care Unit." *Journal of Music Therapy*, 28: 180–92, 1991.

- Cone Wesson, Barbara, et al. "Hearing Sensitivity in Newborns Estimated from ABR's to Bone Conducted Sounds." *Journal of the American Academy of Audiology*, 8: 299–307, 1997.

Chapter 3

Page 45 **" . . . a fetus doesn't start that way!"**: Donovan, B. T., *Hormones and Human Behaviour: The Scientific Basis of Psychiatry*, CUP, Cambridge, 1985. See also Fausto-Sterling, A., *Myths of Gender*, Basic Books, New York, 1985.

Page 50 **3/3/08**: a new study is in the news: "Car crashes are the leading cause of death for tweens and teens, and a new study outlines some of the most dangerous circumstances . . . The study, conducted with State Farm Mutual Automobile Insurance Co., appears in the March edition of *Archives of Pediatrics & Adolescent Medicine*." www.breitbart.com/article. php?id=2008-03-03_D8V680oO2&show_article=1&cat=breaking.

Page 49 **" . . . a famous study . . . of monkeys . . ."**: The long-term studies of testosterone levels and hierarchical behavior in a community of monkeys was carried out by Robert Rose, Department of Psychiatry, Walter Reed Army Institute of Research, Washington; cited in Bahr, Robert, *The Virility Factor*, Longman, New York, 1976.

Page 52 Elium, D., & Elium, J., *Raising a Son: Parents and the Making of a Healthy Man*, Celestial Arts, California, 2004 (3rd ed). Their breakthrough book with its very positive view of boys is well worth reading. It preceded by several years Michael Gurian's better-known book, *The Wonder of Boys*, and covers similar ground with a more humanistic tone.

Page 54 **" . . . boys in scary or violent school environments produced more testosterone"**: Reported by Dr. Rex Stoessiger in Hobart, Australia. Personal communication, May 1997.

Page 55 **" . . . over many generations their jaws and teeth became smaller . . ."**: Flannery, T., *The Future Eaters*, Reed, Melbourne, 1994. This is a superb book for understanding human prehistory, our place in the environment, and what adaptive and maladaptive patterns we bring from the past. It especially focuses on the Australian situation.

Page 58 **" . . . will sexually assault another human being"**: Wyre, R., expert witness, transcripts of the Woods Royal Commission, NSW, 1996. Raymond Wyre is a British specialist in treating sexual abuse offenders. The Woods Royal Commission was set up to investigate police corruption in NSW, Australia, then extended to cover pedophilia in that state. It resulted in extensive public awareness and exposure of pedophilia in schools, government agencies, and the community at large.

Chapter 4

Page 61 **" . . . gender differences are evident in the unborn baby's brain"**: in Kimura, D., "Are men's and women's brains really different?", *Canadian Psychology*, 1987, 28.2, p. 133. "It is probably true that hormones organise the brain early in life, and also true that we see typically distinct patterns of brain organisation in adult men and women." Kimura goes on to add that hormones affect performance throughout life, and that handedness and intelligence also influence how the brain is organized. It is more complex than just gender, though gender is a major influence.

Page 61 "The corpus callosum in boys is proportionately smaller . . .": Neuroanatomist Laura Allen, working at UCLA, found from actual dissection of brains of men and women and children that the corpus callosum is much larger in females. This is the part of the brain that passes information from the logical side of the brain to the intuitive side and back again. This may explain how women can manage to express themselves better, especially about subtle or emotional aspects, as well as their ability to multitask; for example, remembering a shopping list while watching a toddler and talking to a friend in the supermarket.

Men tend to stay in one side of their brain, becoming good at logical or very focused tasks. Kimura told the *Los Angeles Times*: "It used to be accepted that men and women process information the same way. We now know that this is not true. The entire brain is different at a very subtle level, at least."

Page 62 " . . . localized on one part of one side only": Bennett, A., and Shaywitz, Sally E., "Sex Differences in the Functional Organization of the Brain for Language," *Nature*, 1995, pp. 373, 607–9. This study represents a turning point. It was the first major cooperation between many disciplines—from radiology to physics, pediatrics, and neurology—to look at the question of differing brain structure using MRI scans of the brain actually doing thinking tasks. MRI was new, extremely costly, and not without risks to the subjects, and so had not often been carried out prior to this study. I have quoted the abstract in full.

The question of whether there exist sex differences in the functional organization of the brain for language represents an area of considerable debate. A long held, but unconfirmed hypothesis, posits that in general, language functions are more likely to be highly lateralized in males but represented in both cerebral hemispheres in females. Here we use echo-planar functional magnetic resonance imaging (fMRI) to study 38 right-handed subjects (19 males and 19 females) during orthographic (letter recognition), phonological (rhyme) and semantic (semantic category) tasks. We find significant sex differences in activation patterns during phonological tasks: in males, brain activation is localized to left inferior frontal gyrus (IFG) regions; in females the pattern of activation is very different, engaging more diffuse neural systems involving both left and right IFG regions. These data provide the first clear evidence of sex differences in the functional organization of the brain for language and indicate that these differences exist at the level of phonological processing.

Page 64 " . . . help your child avoid learning or language problems . . .": Harasty, J., Double, K., Halliday, G. M., Kril, J. J., McRitchie, D. A., "Language Associated Cortical Regions Are Proportionally Larger in the Female Brain." *Archives of Neurology*, October, 1996. "Our results suggest that women have proportionally larger Wernicke's and Broca's language associated regions compared with men. These anatomical differences may correlate with superior language skills previously demonstrated in women."

Page 70 "They are especially delayed in what is called *fine-motor coordination* . . .": Vann, A. S., "Let's not push our kindergarten kids," Vol. 57, *Education Digest*, 9/1/91, 43 (Courtesy Electric Library). Also, Cratty, B. J., *Perceptual Motor Development in Infants and Children*, Prentice Hall, New Jersey, 1986 (612.65/Crat).

Sex-related differences in motor development are present as early as the preschool years. Boys are slightly advanced over girls in abilities that emphasize force and power. Girls have an edge in fine-motor skills of drawing and penmanship, and in certain gross-motor capacities that combine balance and foot movement such as hopping and skipping. Girls are ahead of boys in overall physical maturity, which may be partly responsible for their better balance and precision of movement.

Only in mid- to late teens, do boys catch up with girls. At this age, boys increase in speed, strength, and endurance athletically, until even the average boy outperforms most girls.

Chapter 5

Page 76 ". . . fathers have increased the time they spend with children . . .": Adrienne Burgess, *Fatherhood Reclaimed*, Vermillion, London, 1997.

Page 83 "If you want to get along with boys, learn to wrestle!": Paul Whyte, Sydney Men's Network, at "Boys in Education" seminar, Hobart, 1994.

Page 85 Biddulph, S., and Biddulph, S., *The Making of Love*, Doubleday, Sydney, 1989.

Page 86 "What fathers do": Copyright © 1992 by Jack Kammer. Jack Kammer is also the author of *Good Will Toward Men* (St. Martin's Press, New York, 1995).

Page 91 "ADD": Jureidini, J., "Debate: attention deficit disorder," *Australian Doctor*, 11 October 1996. Dr. Jureidini is a pediatrician who seriously doubts the validity of ADD as a separate condition. Even Dr. Gordon Serfontein, who pioneered the concept of ADD in Australia, writes in his original book that the absence of fathers is a very large component in the problems associated with ADD. He urges fathers to get involved in playing with, and teaching self-control to, their sons.

Page 95 "The research supporting the importance of dads is overwhelmingly clear": Blankenhorn. D., *Fatherless America*, Basic Books, New York, 1995. Blankenhorn's book is statistically well researched, and makes a powerful case, especially for the United States, where 40 percent of children do not have their father in the home. Low attainment at school, teen pregnancy, juvenile crime convictions, learning difficulties and school drop-out rates, as well as domestic violence and sexual abuse of children, are all higher in families where the birth father is no longer present. His conclusions are less convincing—that we must "make" fathers be more responsible. He doesn't understand that men want to be good fathers.

Children ideally need a man and a woman who are lovingly invested and committed to them. Single mothers can raise children well, lesbian couples can raise children well, but whenever I talk to single mothers or lesbian parents, they are acutely aware of the need for same-sex role models for their sons, and most take active steps to organize these, against considerable difficulties. Having a real, live father on the spot is clearly the best arrangement if he is a halfway-reasonable, safe, and caring man.

Chapter 6

Page 108 "Testicles are very sensitive . . .": Acknowledgments to Dr. Nick Cooling of the University of Tasmania for verifying and expanding this advice.

Page 113 Cookbooks for kids: Here are some suggestions:

The Everything Kids' Cookbook (Nissenberg, Adams, 2002)

New Junior Cookbook (Better Homes and Gardens, 2004)

The River Cottage Family Cookbook (Fearnley-Whittingstall and Carr, Ten Speed Press, 2008)

Page 118 Introducing a New Partner: *The Wonder of Boys*, Michael Gurian, Tarcher/Putnam, New York, 1996.

Chapter 7

Page 130 "Robert Bly calls it a 'sibling society' . . .": Bly, Robert, *The Sibling Society*, Vintage, 1997.

Page 136 " . . . 'gender identity disorder' . . .": Soutter, Alison, "A longitudinal study of three cases of gender identity disorder of childhood successfully resolved in the school setting," *School Psychology International*, vol. 17, 1996, pp. 49–57.

Page 140 Billy Connolly: Connolly, Billy, *World Tour of Australia*, BBC Books, London, 1996.

Page 142 The Joy of Sex: Comfort, Alex, *The Joy of Sex*, Quartet Press, London, 1974.

Page 144 " . . . many youth suicides are actually caused by youngsters discovering they are gay": In "Being gay is a big factor in youth suicides," Debra Jopson (*Sydney Morning Herald*, 26 February 1997) referred to the large-scale research of Dr. Gary Remafedi at University of Minnesota, which found that 30 percent of gay adolescent boys said they had tried to kill themselves. Risk factors were "coming out" at an early age, substance abuse, and displaying effeminate behavior.

Chapter 8

Page 149 "So it's vital that we get more men into primary school teaching": There is clearly a recruitment problem in schools today. Many school principals are quite aware of these needs and compete to attract trained men of the right type, especially in primary schools. Many teachers tell me the problem is teacher training—that they got little in the way of classroom skills or relevant practice from their university courses, and that this lack of skills means they become overwhelmed and repressive in the classroom in order to cope.

And it doesn't help that boys come to school so under-fathered that they have no self-control or inner calmness, and the teacher's day is spent doing crowd control.

Just 21 percent of the nation's 3 million teachers are men, according to the National Education Association (NEA). Over the past two decades, the ratio of men to women in the classroom has steadily declined. Today, it stands at a 40-year low ("Needed in Class: A few good men," *Christian Science Monitor*, March 15, 2005. www.csmonitor.com/2005/0315/p11s01-legn.html). Clearly, we have to take steps to bring more men into teaching. Two steps might be better pay and better training (including accelerated training for mature-age entry to encourage men thirty years and over to enter teaching from other careers).

Page 149 "Lack of defensiveness . . . in a way that doesn't issue a challenge . . .": The tendency of male teachers to get "hormonally" stirred up when teaching boys who threaten them has an amusing and probably comparable parallel in work with primates. "Adolescent male chimps in the facility test recruits by spitting water, banging on cages and similar stunts. Deborah Fouts reports that women survive the initiation at a rate of 3 to 1 over men because women ignore the antics, just as they would a two-year-old acting out; men tend to get impatient, react to the provocation, and escalate the chimps' rampages." Reported in Vines, *Raging Hormones*.

Page 150 "Recent studies have found that . . . boys . . . really *do* want to be successful . . .": Hudson & Carr, "Ending Alienation."

Page 153 Ireland, Peter, *Boys in Schools*, Fletcher & Browne, Finch Publishing, Sydney, 1995.

Page 160 "The largest study . . . of bullying in schools": Nansel and Overpeck's report cites 17 percent of children describe themselves as being bullied frequently. Around one-third of these also report that they themselves bully other children. Around 10 percent of students admit that they themselves bully others but are not bullied themselves. Nansel and Overpeck, *Journal of the American Medical Association*, April 25 2001.

Whole school programs to reduce bullying are described in Garrett, A., *Bullying in American Schools* (McFarland, 2003) and Coloroso, B., *The Bully, the Bullied and the Bystander* (HarperResource, 2004), along with the research backing for what works best.

Page 164 " . . . there is one way to firm up your self-image . . .": Stoessiger, R., "Boys and Literacy—an equity issue." Accessible at the Manhood Online website: www.manhood.com.au.

Page 166 "What parents can do": Adapted from *Bullying in Schools and What to Do About It*, Rigby, Ken, published by ACER, Canberra, 1996.

Page 170 "Listen to this boy describing his sensory problems": "What is it like to be autistic?" Darren White, *Autism Spectrum Disorder*, Autistic Association of NSW, Sydney, 1992.

Page 172 ". . . Ashfield principal Ann King . . .": "Mid-school Crisis" in *Sydney Morning Herald*, 17 February 1997, p. 12.

Chapter 9

Page 184 " . . . parents guard against 'sports abuse' . . .": Messner, Michael, *Power at Play: Sports and the Problem of Masculinity*, Beacon Press, Boston, 1992.

Page 185 Richard Fletcher: Lecture to Men's Health and Wellbeing Association (NSW) Open Day, November 1996, Sydney.

Page 185 " . . . two thousand of these injuries": *Sydney Morning Herald*. Team sports accounted for 75 percent of all sports injuries in Australia. The most dangerous category of sports included rugby league and rugby union. The second most dangerous category included Australian rules football, grass skiing, boxing, ice hockey, parachuting, skateboard riding, and snow skiing. The third most dangerous group included hockey and cycling. The fourth included basketball, cricket, gymnastics, netball, soccer, squash, and touch football.

Appendix A

Page 199 Mate, Gabor, *Scattered: How Attention Deficit Disorder Originates, and What You Can Do About It*, Plume, 2000.

The Pediatric Advisory Committee of the Food and Drug Administration released a statement on June 30, 2005 identifying two possible safety concerns regarding Concerta and other brands of methylphenidate: psychiatric adverse effects and cardiovascular adverse effects. Ritalin and other stimulant drugs are now required to carry a strong "black box warning."

Chromosome abnormalities were discovered in a small-scale investigation that is not yet validated in a large-scale controlled study. "Cytogenetic effects in children treated with methylphenidate," *Cancer Letters*, 18 Dec 2005, 230 (2).

Appendix B

Page 203 This list was devised by Deborah Hartman and Richard Fletcher, Boys to Fine Men Program, University of Newcastle, New South Wales. To learn more about this program, visit www.newcastle.edu.au/centre/fac/binsp/index.html.

Index